Literary Feasts

1230 Avenue of the Americas
New York, NY 10020

ISBN-13: 978-0-7432-8828-6
ISBN-10: 0-7432-8828-9

First Atria Books hardcover edition February 2006

This book was conceived,
designed, and produced by:
THE IVY PRESS LIMITED
The Old Candlemakers, West Street,
Lewes, East Sussex, BN7 2NZ, UK.

CREATIVE DIRECTOR Peter Bridgewater
PUBLISHER Sophie Collins
EDITORIAL DIRECTOR Jason Hook
SENIOR PROJECT EDITOR Hazel Songhurst
ART DIRECTOR Karl Shanahan
ILLUSTRATOR Sarah Young

1 3 5 7 9 10 8 6 4 2

Manufactured in China

SEAN BRAND

Literary Feasts

INSPIRED EATING FROM CLASSIC FICTION

ATRIA BOOKS
New York London Toronto Sydney

Contents

INTRODUCTION

Have you ever wanted to cook like Epicurus or eat like the giant Gargantua? Does James Bond conjure up visions of stone crabs and Dom Perignon rather than Aston Martins and Halle Berry? The bestseller lists are topped by cookbooks, and some of the most famous people in the world today are well known just because they can cook. Only the rarest amateur chef will risk a recipe that hasn't been given the seal of approval by Martha Stewart, Delia Smith, or Nigella Lawson. But our actual choice of meals is dwindling to the prepackaged, predigested fare that the supermarkets would like us to have, or the same-in-Kansas-and-Kamchatka fast-food offerings from McDonalds. If you are tired of dull, predictable, twenty-first century food, you are now holding the only cookbook you will ever need. *Literary Feasts* provides the inspiration for new eating experiences from the greatest works of literature ever written.

It really is extraordinary how much time the most famous characters in literature spend eating food, or thinking about food, or occasionally—in the case of Miss Havisham in Charles Dickens' *Great Expectations*—preserving it for decades. Even angels recognize this: when Raphael comes to chat with Adam about predestination, free will, and so on in John Milton's *Paradise Lost*, they meet over lunch served by Eve. This is probably the earliest example of topless waitressing in the literary canon.

English poet and playwright Wilfred Gibson's soldiers eat lying on their backs while watching the shells fly overhead. Ebenezer Scrooge's way of making up for his meanness in Dickens's *A Christmas Carol* is to offer his employees a festive spread. Algernon Moncrieff's response to impending disaster in Oscar Wilde's *The Importance of Being Earnest* is to eat English muffins. In short, the books all say that food is important.

~ LITERARY APPETITES ~

Why is there so much food in your average great work of literature? Well, for one thing, what people eat can create a scene and a set of characters beautifully in the reader's mind. You only need to hear James Bond's advice on cocktails (shaken not stirred) to realize that you are in the presence of a man with refined tastes about which he is very particular. Meals also bring characters together at critical moments in the plot—picnics provide turning points in Jane Austen's *Emma* as well as in E.M. Forster's *A Room with a View*. For epicureans, the whiff of the food they eat, and the beverages they consume, are as evocative as any amount of dialogue.

Particularly literate readers will be aware that some meals are missing from this book. We admit this readily: reasons of space sadly dictate that you will find no sign of the perversely orgiastic feasts in the Marquis de Sade's *120 Days of Sodom,* or Ernest Hemingway's rabbit stew in *For Whom the Bell Tolls*. But the book contains a great deal else to whet the palate.

And before we set to sharpening knives and skimming the court-bouillon, let us salute the most food-obsessed work of literature in the canon. Parson James Woodforde's extraordinary diaries, which he kept throughout his adult life from the eighteenth century into the nineteenth, describe nearly every meal he ate in the most gratifying detail. Oddly for a clergyman, he almost never mentions God. This is one of his better efforts, from the evening of 20 April 1796:

"Dinner was announced soon after our arrival, which consisted of the following things, Salmon boiled & Shrimp Sauce some White Soup, Saddle of Mutton rosted & Cucumber &c., Lambs Fry, Tongue, Breast of Veal ragoued, rice Pudding, the best part of a Rump of Beef stewed immediately after the Salmon was removed. 2nd course. A Couple of Spring Chicken, rosted Sweetbreads, Jellies, Maccaroni, frill'd Oysters, 2 small Crabs, & made Dish of Eggs... We got home about half past nine, a we went very slowly on Account of Briton's walking, who... was very imprudent indeed, but I believe he had been making too free with Mr Mellish's Beer &c."

~ COOKING THE BOOKS ~

These *Literary Feasts* are divided into the regular meals of breakfast, lunch, tea, and dinner, plus sections on eating outdoors, children's food, and special occasions. There is also a list of recommended reading at the end of the book, which might help you take the literary inspiration for eating and cooking a little further. Each section offers a series of books to inspire you, putting the work and the author in some kind of context, and lists the essential ingredients—not just for the food, but for the authentic atmosphere too. We have also devised a rating system that can help you work out just what these meals are intended to achieve—whether they err toward the taste or toward the ambience—and in some cases to let you know it might be wisest not to put them in your mouth at all.

THE RATING SYSTEM

LITERARY MERIT

A GOOD READ · UNPUTDOWNABLE · WELL-THUMBED CLASSIC

FOOD QUALITY

BARELY EDIBLE · DELICIOUS · POISONOUS

COMPANY

CONVIVIAL · LONELY · DOWNRIGHT DANGEROUS

TABLE FOR...

TÊTE À TÊTE · HAPPY GATHERING · BANQUET

BREAKFAST

THE PICKWICK PAPERS

If there was one writer who was obsessed with breakfast, it was Charles Dickens. While some of the other meals are glossed over in his voluminous novels, breakfast is always described lovingly—and if the meal is not actually portrayed in detail, we are always assured that his characters have started the day the way nutritionists recommend. Of all the varieties of breakfast, it is the "wedding breakfast" that has a place closest to Dickens's heart. Before 1880, the laws of England stipulated that weddings must take place in the morning, and it was customary for the bride, bridegroom, and guests to leave the church after the ceremony and move straight on to breakfast.

YOU WILL NEED

- A BRIDE AND GROOM
- MINCE PIES
- A CHRISTMAS CAKE
- A BEVY OF EXCITABLE YOUNG RELATIVES AND SERVANTS
- A SUPPLY OF HANDKERCHIEFS
- A VERY GREAT DEAL OF WINE
- WEDDING CLOTHES
- LEATHER BOOTS

WEDDING BREAKFASTS

If you are planning your nuptials, the wedding breakfast in Dickens's first novel *The Pickwick Papers* is a fine model to follow for entertaining your guests. Originally published in installments in 1836, it follows the adventures of the eponymous hero, Mr. Pickwick, and his two friends as they engage in a constant defense of dignity and search for true love. Mr. Pickwick presides over the occasion of the wedding at Dingley Dell, of his farmer friend Mr. Wardle's daughter Isabella to Mr. Trundle, who appears over and over again in the book, but never says anything. This particular breakfast includes cake, mince pies—it was just after Christmas—a very great deal of wine, and some lachrymose speeches, after which the guests depart on a twenty-mile walk to prepare themselves for the next meal.

A GOOD READ DELICIOUS CONVIVIAL
BANQUET

~ DICKENSIAN ROLE-PLAY ~

Eating breakfast in Dickensian style is a surefire recipe for a successful wedding party. There is enough alcoholic bonhomie to guarantee your reputation as a host, the bridesmaids are always gorgeous and black-eyed, and the meal enormous—and usually followed shortly afterward by a similar one. Some top-drawer sentimentality is also required in the after-breakfast speeches. But there are other darker or more unusual examples of the Dickensian breakfast.

1) THE SOCIETY WEDDING

The wedding breakfast, complete with ornamental gold and silver camels on the table, is not such a comfortable affair in Dickens's last finished novel, *Our Mutual Friend* (1864–65). Here the meal is presided over by the ghastly Lady Tippins, the widow of a man knighted by mistake for somebody else. Moral of the story, as Dickens said in various places: "Better is a dinner of herbs where love is than a stalled ox and hatred withal" (Proverbs 15:17).

2) THE STALE BREAKFAST

The most unpleasant wedding breakfast in all literature is undoubtedly Miss Havisham's, which remains laid out and uneaten on the table in Dickens's *Great Expectations* (1860–61) some decades after she was jilted at the altar. This event sent her mad, and she remains in her bridal dress, still looking at the breakfast, many years later. The Havisham breakfast has little to recommend it in terms of palatability, but it certainly has atmosphere.

"The most prominent object was a long table with a tablecloth spread on it, as if a feast had been in preparation when the house and the clocks all stopped together. An epergne or centrepiece of some kind was in the middle of this cloth; it was so heavily overhung with cobwebs that its form was quite undistinguishable; and, as I looked along the yellow expanse out of which I remember its seeming to grow, like a black fungus, I saw speckled-legged spiders with blotchy bodies running home to it, and running out from it."

3) THE MENACING BREAKFAST

Of all Dickens's breakfasts, the one eaten by the unpleasant Mr. Quilp in *The Old Curiosity Shop* (1840) must be the most disturbing. Be careful with this one: the Quilp breakfast involves swallowing boiled eggs in their shells and whole prawns, heads and all. This is useful for houseguests who have outstayed their welcome.

"He ate hard eggs, shell and all, devoured gigantic prawns with the heads and tails on, chewed tobacco and water-cresses at the same time and with extraordinary greediness, drank boiling tea without winking, bit his fork and spoon till they bent again."

KIDNAPPED

THE plot for *Kidnapped* (1886) leapt into Robert Louis Stevenson's head when he was reading a description of a murder trial in Edinburgh, Scotland. It is the tale of a young man, David Balfour, who is kidnapped by his miserly uncle and stolen away to sea. Breakfast in the Highlands of Scotland turns out to be a startling and recurrent concoction, consisting almost entirely of porridge, served by David's uncle when he first introduces himself.

~ ALL-DAY BREAKFAST ~

There are three elements to this meal: a large pot of porridge eaten with horn spoons, some beer, and a tobacco pipe. In a possibly ungenerous demonstration of the Scottish characteristic of thrift, the same pot of porridge is reheated for lunch and for dinner the same day. If you are a creature of simple habits, or have recently come into a large supply of oatmeal, this might be of interest to you. But it helps if one guest harbors bitter resentments toward the other—and for the recipient to be entirely ignorant of these powerful feelings. For authenticity's sake, the *Kidnapped* meal needs to end with an unpleasant surprise.

YOU WILL NEED

- A LARGE BLACK POT
- CONGEALED PORRIDGE
- A CLAY PIPE WITH TOBACCO
- A LONELY, ANCIENT STONE MANOR WITH BROKEN WINDOW PANES
- A GLOOMY, MISERLY, AND SUSPICIOUS ATTITUDE
- A NIGHTCAP AND POWDERED WIG

"I made the best of my own way back to the kitchen,
where he had lit the fire and was making porridge.
The table was laid with two bowls and two horn spoons,
but the same single measure of small beer.
Perhaps my eye rested on this particular with some surprise…
for he spoke up as if in answer to my thought,
asking me if I would like to drink ale—for so he called it.
I told him such was my habit, but not to put himself about.
'Na, na,' said he; 'I'll deny you nothing in reason.'"

Cold Comfort Farm

The journalist Stella Gibbons was working on London's *Evening Standard* newspaper in the 1930s when she took against the then hugely popular genre of rural melodrama. Writers like Mary Webb churned out novels such as *Precious Bane* which were passionate, morbid, and ridiculous in equal amounts. Gibbons decided to write her own commonsense version, and *Cold Comfort Farm* (1932) was the result. The book describes the arrival of brisk, sensible Flora Poste at the unspeakable farm populated by her distant relatives the Starkadders, and her relentless efforts to reform them. These efforts culminate in the reclusive matriarch of the household, damaged at an early age by seeing "something nasty in the woodshed," embarking on a world cruise. But they start with breakfast.

~ PORRIDGE AGAIN ~

Breakfast at Cold Comfort Farm features copious amounts of burned porridge, spread liberally over the table during the frequently violent family arguments. Flora offends the elderly retainer Adam Lambsbreath, who is the provider of this delicacy, by refusing the porridge on her first morning and requesting bread, butter, and tea, thus striking a blow for modernity.

Having asked for a corner of the table, and a piece of newspaper to protect her from the flying lumps of porridge, Flora signals her firm intention to change things. As well as feeding the hungry farmworkers, the porridge also measures the emotional intensity of the action, boiling over at pivotal moments during the narrative. A better example of the significance of food in literature you could not wish to find. Even so, there may be inspiration in the original breakfast, if only to conjure up a certain view of English rural life toward the middle of the twentieth century.

YOU WILL NEED

- A FARMHOUSE (FILTHY) WITH STONE FLAGSTONES (UNBRUSHED)
- A CAULDRON OF PORRIDGE
- RUMORS OF BREAD, BUTTER, AND TEA
- TURNIP FOR SLICING
- A COLD DRAFT
- LEATHER JERKINS
- SOMETHING NASTY IN THE WOODSHED

UNPUTDOWNABLE DELICIOUS CONVIVIAL

HAPPY GATHERING (ALTHOUGH ONE AT A TIME)

LUNCH

PARADISE LOST

IT isn't every day that you have the opportunity to sit down to lunch with a six-winged angel, but this is the guest whom Adam and Eve entertain in the Garden of Eden in John Milton's epic poem *Paradise Lost* (1667). The archangel Raphael has been sent by God to remind the original human beings that they are living a blissful existence that is threatened by the deceit of Satan. Raphael's arrival takes Adam and Eve by surprise—but fortunately they are able to rustle up something to eat from a vast array of fruits and fruit juices.

YOU WILL NEED

- FRUIT TREES IN ABUNDANCE
- AN ACRE OR SO OF PARADISE,
- JUICY GOURDS (BUT FOR GOODNESS SAKE DON'T EAT THE APPLES)
- OPTIONAL FIG LEAVES
- A CHANCE OF ATTRACTING AN ANGEL
- A SERPENT

ORIGINAL SIN

We are not yet at the point of Original Sin, but it's reasonable to claim this as the original lunch party. Raphael is, after all, a "sociable spirit" according to Milton. Eve prepares "Savourie fruits, of taste to please/True appetite, and not disrelish thirst/Of nectarous draughts between, /From milkie stream, Berrie, or Grape." Raphael's advice unfortunately does them no good, but the scene is inspiring and the meal worth repeating. This is not just because of the nudity. The whole business of eating *al fresco* is close to paradise.

"Mean while at Table EVE
Ministerd naked, and their flowing cups
With pleasant liquors crown'd: O innocence
Deserving Paradise! if ever, then,
Then had the Sons of God excuse to have bin
Enamour'd at that sight; but in those hearts
Love unlibidinous reign'd, nor jealousie
Was understood, the injur'd Lovers Hell."

  WELL-THUMBED CLASSIC  DELICIOUS ❤ CONVIVIAL  TÊTE À TÊTE

Tom Jones

When Henry Fielding's classic novel *The History of Tom Jones, a Foundling* (1749) was made into a movie by Tony Richardson in 1963, the erotic lunch scene became one of the most famous in cinema history. In the book more is left to the imagination. Even so, the writing certainly leads you in the right direction. The novel watches the rise and near demise of Tom before he suddenly finds he is an heir after all. The erotic lunch sees handsome Tom and Mrs. Waters—a lady of a certain age who he has just rescued—eat in a fashion that leaves no doubt that after devouring the food they intend to leap into bed and devour each other.

AMOROUS EATING

Tom Jones has been on the road for some time before this welcome meal, having been framed for a breach of discipline and taste he did not commit back in his adopted household. So before allowing himself to be seduced by Mrs. Waters he has to satisfy the needs of his stomach. This is an important lesson: if we are hungry, then we have to fortify ourselves with at least "an excellent sirloin of beef or a bottle of burgundy," as Richardson says, before we can get down to anything else. So be patient: there is no point in ruining a good evening by taking offense because your partner has to take on fuel before attending to your libidinous requirements.

YOU WILL NEED

- A QUIET CORNER OF A BAR
- LARGE QUANTITIES OF BEEF AND BOTTLED BEER
- A WET AND PASSIONATE EATING STYLE (BUT BE CAREFUL NOT TO DISGUST YOUR FELLOW GUEST)
- A SMOLDERING LOOK
- SOMEWHERE PRIVATE TO GO IMMEDIATELY YOU HAVE FINISHED EATING

"Three pounds at least of that flesh which formerly had contributed to the composition of an ox was now honoured with becoming part of the individual Mr Jones."

 WELL-THUMBED CLASSIC  DELICIOUS  CONVIVIAL TÊTE À TÊTE

~ TOM JONES ROLE-PLAY ~

Tom Jones is a novel that includes a great deal of eating—the eighteenth century was the Golden Age of overeating—and a great deal of more or less illicit passion. The description of Tom gorging himself on an ox while Mrs. Waters makes eyes at him across the table is a neat way of confusing the two. As Fielding explains in the book, as a kind of apology for writing too much about a meal, "the act of eating… must be in some measure performed [even] by the greatest prince, heroe, or philosopher upon earth." The Tom Jones meal is for people who enjoy putting lovely things in their mouths.

BON APPETIT

This is a meal that is all about satisfying appetite—for lunch as well as for lust—so don't be afraid to show you are enjoying it. Successful seduction requires an enthusiastic approach.

"The fair one, enraged by her frequent disappointments, determined on a short cessation of arms. Which interval she employed in making ready every engine of amorous warfare for the renewing of the attack when dinner should be over."

HEARTS AND MOUTHS

Yes, you can seduce your guest by the way you eat, tearing, slurping, and guzzling with verve. But don't go too far: one woman's lusty slathering is another's disgusting drooling—possibly even the same person at different times of the day.

"How much soever we may be in love with an excellent sirloin of beef, or bottle of Burgundy; with a damask rose, or Cremona fiddle; yet do we never smile, nor ogle, nor dress, nor flatter, nor endeavour by any other arts or tricks to gain the affection of the said beef &c."

SIGHS MATTERS

What convinces Tom Jones that this meal is about more than simply food is the positive barrage of erotic sighing directed at him by his eating partner. But remember, you have to stop guzzling for a moment just to be able to hear such subtleties.

"A sigh which none could have heard unmoved... had it not luckily been driven from his ears by the coarse bubbling of some bottled ale, which at that time he was pouring forth."

LITTLE WOMEN

THERE was obviously something in the water of Concord, Massachusetts. The town seemed to breed philosophers and writers: Emerson, Thoreau, and of course Louisa May Alcott, the daughter of a philosopher herself. After a brief stint nursing in the American Civil War, she made her name and fortune with her novel *Little Women* (1868), a semi-autobiographical account of sisters growing up in a very similar town. There is a lunch party at the heart of the book to entertain a young man, which the heroine Jo cooks disastrously. All the guests have the misfortune of tasting her fruit salad, which is sweetened with salt and served with cream that has been allowed to go sour. If cooking is not your forte, then take heart from this example.

YOU WILL NEED

- LOBSTER
- BURNED TOAST
- LUMPY BLANCMANGE
- SALT FOR THE FRUIT SALAD (BUT GO EASY IF YOU ARE REALLY EATING IT)
- A DEAD BUDGERIGAR
- STARCHED PETTICOATS AND LONG DRESSES
- A SENSE OF HUMOR

~ LUMPY BLANCMANGE ~

The lunch day begins with the death of the family pet bird. Perhaps Jo should have taken this as a warning and stayed in bed. Her asparagus disintegrates at one end while the stalks stay hard and the potatoes are undercooked. The blancmange is lumpy, and the business of the fruit and cream ends when her sister Amy takes a mouthful, chokes, covers her face, and flees. However, the point of this literary feast is to show how to behave in the face of such culinary misfortune. Jo and her guests fill up on bread, butter, and olives and laugh the whole thing off.

"The bread burnt black; for the salad-dressing so aggravated her, that she let everything else go till she had convinced herself that she could not make it fit to eat. The lobster was a scarlet mystery to her, but she hammered and poked, till it was unshelled, and its meager proportions concealed in a grove of lettuce-leaves."

WELL-THUMBED CLASSIC • BARELY EDIBLE
CONVIVIAL • HAPPY GATHERING

BRIDESHEAD REVISITED

EVELYN WAUGH's most famous novel *Brideshead Revisited* (1945) is a nostalgic exposition of forbidden love and Catholicism, but it begins among the outrageous aesthetes of Oxford University in the 1920s at an extraordinary lunch party in Christ Church, a college by the River Isis. Here we are introduced to the mildly camp Sebastian Flyte, the teddy-bear hugging son of a member of the Roman Catholic aristocracy, and the outrageously camp Anthony Blanche, in a chocolate suit and a large bow-tie. At the end of the party, Blanche stands on the balcony with a megaphone, languidly reciting T.S. Eliot's then-shocking poem "The Waste Land" to the rowers returning from the river. This was based on a real incident when the future art critic Harold Acton did precisely that, in order to "excite rage in the hearts of the Philistines."

YOU WILL NEED

- LOBSTER
- CHAMPAGNE
- A PÂTÉ OF PLOVERS' EGGS NESTING IN MOSS
- A SMATTERING OF JEUNESSE DORÉE
- A MEGAPHONE
- FLANNELS AND BLAZERS
- SOME BOOKS OF SHOCKINGLY MODERN VERSE

WONDERFUL THINGS

Waugh provides few details about the lunch itself, except that it consists mainly of a large plate of plovers' eggs, sent by Sebastian Flyte's mother from the stately home where she lives, and lobster. This lunch also involves a certain amount of champagne. Apart from that, you will have to fill in the gaps with your imagination and the stock of your nearest deli. In the book the lunch is an entirely male affair, but you may feel that this is taking things too far. Inviting some female guests will not spoil the atmosphere. What is absolutely essential, however, is that innocent bystanders should be force-fed modern poetry. *Ars gratia artis*—"art for art's sake."

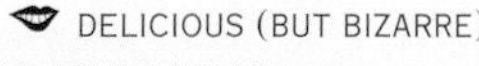

TEA

ALICE'S ADVENTURES IN WONDERLAND

LEWIS CARROLL, the author of *Alice's Adventures in Wonderland* (1865)—which includes one of the most famous tea parties in literature—was the pen name of a shy mathematician from Christ Church, Oxford, with an interest in photography and a peculiar inability to make friends with anyone except little girls. The book tells the story of Alice's adventures following her fall down a rabbit hole. The delightful lunacy at the heart of Alice's experiences was such that Queen Victoria demanded copies of all Carroll's other books. Imagine Her Majesty's dismay, dear reader, when a package arrived containing a series of mathematical treatises. Alice meets the Mad Hatter and his guests—the March Hare and the Dormouse—out of doors at a table set for a rather larger tea party. No food is in evidence and tea is the only nourishment on offer. The table talk is pure nonsense. The resulting transaction is more surreal than meal, but it could never be left out of a book of literary meals.

YOU WILL NEED

- A LARGE TABLE SET FOR TEA
- A COMMODIOUS TEAPOT
- A HATTER OF DOUBTFUL SANITY
- A STORE OF RIDDLES (ANSWERS UNNECESSARY)
- A DORMOUSE
- A LARGE FOB-WATCH

EAT ME

The reason for the extra place settings is that there is never time to wash up the dishes, so the guests simply move on to another plate when they have finished with the previous one. This practice will be familiar to anyone who has shared a student house and can be usefully adopted if the dishwasher breaks down. The menu is limited, which makes it easy to prepare, and to match the bizarre nature of the original conversation, you should try inviting your friends round for the Mad Hatter meal after a convivial evening in a bar.

UNPUTDOWNABLE · BARELY EDIBLE (NO FOOD IS FORTHCOMING)
CONVIVIAL (IN A MAD WAY) · HAPPY GATHERING (WITH PLACES TO SPARE)

À la Recherche du Temps Perdu

Snobbish, self-obsessed, and fussy, Marcel Proust published the first volume of his enormous semi-autobiographical novel sequence *À la Recherche du Temps Perdu* (*The Remembrance of Times Past*) at his own expense in 1913, having been turned down by respectable publishers. He never quite finished the seven-volume sequence before he died nine years later, scribbling away in his soundproofed flat in the rue Hausmann, in Paris. Proust's masterpiece is a rambling, stream-of-consciousness achievement, and getting to the end of it marks the pinnacle of some people's reading careers. And all this writing comes from the fleeting memory of sitting down to tea, decades before.

~ Swann's Way of Tea ~

Strictly speaking, the meal that the narrator is remembering in Swann's Way is more like brunch than tea, because it takes place in the morning, on his way to church. But still, it is a snack with tea and that definitely puts it in the tea category. It is also the memory of the experience rather than the experience itself, which puts this recipe at one remove at least from reality. Is it the original tea with his aunt in Combray that we should be following, or is it the tea the narrator has with his mother years later—having forgotten all about Combray, aunt, and her paid companion—that brings it all flooding back? You see how Swann's particular way starts to contort your thought processes into tangled knots.

YOU WILL NEED

- MADELEINE CAKE
- LIMEFLOWER INFUSION
- A TEASPOON
- A SMALL ROOM IN A FRENCH SUBURB
- A DREAMY, NOSTALGIC DISPOSITION
- A TIGHT SUIT AND A LONG, HIGH-NECKED DRESS
- AN AUNT

"And once I had recognized the taste of the crumb of madeleine soaked in her decoction of lime-flowers which my aunt used to give me (although I did not yet know and must long postpone the discovery of why this memory made me so happy) immediately the old gray house upon the street where her room was, rose up like the scenery of a theatre to attach itself to the little pavilion, opening on to the garden."

WELL-THUMBED CLASSIC · DELICIOUS · LONELY · TÊTE À TÊTE

~ PROUST ROLE-PLAY ~

This is not a difficult meal to reproduce. The food itself is so simple that it hardly counts as a meal at all. But the atmosphere is everything: fleeting, obsessive, and slightly unhealthy. If that makes Swann's Aunt Léonie and her infusion sound like an unattractive proposition, don't forget the enormous effect it had on at least one sensitive soul. And who knows, if Swann's aunt's madeleine cake, dissolved in a spoonful of tisane, can bring back the past authentically to him, imagine what it could do for you.

MADELEINE

Madeleine, a cake made from butter and shaped like a scallop, was actually invented by one of Talleyrand's pastry chefs in 1814. It did not therefore have even a century of tradition behind it before Swann dissolved his in the teaspoon to bring back the remembrance of times past. No other cake will do.

"And soon, mechanically, weary after a dull day with the prospect of a depressing morrow, I raised to my lips a spoonful of the tea in which I had soaked a morsel of the cake."

INFUSION

Once you have the authentic cake, you need something to dip it in. Limeflower tea in a small teaspoon is the ideal. Peppermint tea is acceptable. Hot toddy might be worth a try.

"Presently my aunt was able to dip in the boiling infusion, in which she would relish the savor of dead or faded blossom, a little madeleine, of which she would hold out a piece to me when it was sufficiently soft."

SERIOUS NOSTALGIA

Of all the feasts in this book, Swann's way is the most obsessively sensitive and gratuitously nostalgic. It is not about flavor, and certainly not about portion size—it is only a small mouthful that sets Swann off on his multi-volume reverie. This tea reminds the serious gastronome of the exquisite pleasures of simple things simply done, and the extraordinary range of memories than can be revived by simple tastes.

"No sooner had the warm liquid, and the crumbs with it, touched my palate than a shudder ran through my whole body, and I stopped, intent upon the extraordinary changes that were taking place."

The Importance of Being Earnest

What is it about cucumber sandwiches? They have very little taste apart from cleansing the palate. It probably takes more energy to eat them than you can possibly derive from their caloric value. Yet for some reason, it was cucumber sandwiches that were the *sine qua non* of the upper-class English tea at the end of the Victorian age. But cucumbers in Oscar Wilde's play *The Importance of Being Earnest* (1895) are simply a curtain-raiser before the teacakes and muffins that are to follow. The play's action concerns Earnest's unknown origins, and the enormous obstacle this places in the path of his marrying. Wilde's play, which redoubled his reputation as a mercurial genius just months before the sex scandal that was to destroy him, is set almost entirely at a series of different teas.

~ The Importance of Muffins ~

The play opens amidst a flurry of cucumber sandwiches. Like their creator, the two main characters have their guilty secrets. Algernon and Jack both have alternative personas that they adopt to escape from London or to avoid invitations. Their attempts to woo the two girls of the play, and their encounter with the fearsome Lady Bracknell, all take place over tea. In Act II, the cucumbers are replaced by English muffins, just as the two girls discover the truth and break off their engagements. The muffins allow a singular display of English sangfroid.

YOU WILL NEED

- CUCUMBER SANDWICHES
- MUFFINS
- TEACAKES
- A WITTY TURN OF PHRASE
- A SILVER TEAPOT
- WHALEBONE CORSETS, WAISTCOATS, AND TIGHT-FITTING JACKETS
- THE ABILITY TO SAY "A HANDBAG?" IN A QUAVERING VOICE

"I can't eat muffins in an agitated manner.
The butter would probably get on my cuffs.
One should always eat muffins quite calmly.
It is the only way to eat them."

UNPUTDOWNABLE DELICIOUS
CONVIVIAL HAPPY GATHERING (WITH SOME TENSION)

DINNER

THE LEGEND OF SLEEPY HOLLOW

WASHINGTON IRVING wrote this quintessentially American ghost story when he was actually living in the English city of Birmingham. It was published as a short story in his collection *The Sketch Book of Geoffrey Crayon, Gent* (1819). Perhaps it was because he was thousands of miles away from home, and nostalgic for the dawning days of the American republic a generation before, that he lavished so much care on this tale—especially the description of the fateful banquet in a Dutch settlement in upstate New York at the end of the previous century. It is fateful because it is here that a rather priggish Connecticut schoolteacher called Ichabod Crane—who is putting a great deal of effort into wooing the daughter of the house—first hears the terrifying legend of Sleepy Hollow and its ghost.

YOU WILL NEED

- PIES AND PRESERVED FRUITS
- HAM, BEEF, CHICKEN, MILK, AND CREAM
- TEA
- THE MOST VENERABLE MUSICIAN YOU CAN FIND
- A STORE OF MACABRE STORIES
- SPACE FOR WILD DANCING
- AN HEIRESS

Irving spends most of the story telling us all about Sleepy Hollow and it is clear that he doesn't think much of Ichabod Crane, though he is understanding about the fact that food seems to have the same effect on him as alcohol does on everyone else.

*"In his devouring mind's eye,
he pictured to himself every roasting-pig
running about with a pudding in his belly,
and an apple in his mouth..."*

UNPUTDOWNABLE DELICIOUS

CONVIVIAL (IF A LITTLE SCHEMING)  BANQUET

In the end Ichabod is frightened off by the specter of the headless horseman and his rival in love triumphs. If you are planning to use this occasion for the same purpose, you will need to visit the costume store as well as the grocery store. However, you could just let your guests enjoy the fine array of Dutch cakes from the Van Tassel Mansion, the spread of pies of all kinds, the preserved fruits, and the roast chickens—not to mention the cabaret, for which you will need an ancient violinist whose instrument has only three strings still in working order.

SPECTRAL SUPPER

Rounding off the evening with a few ghost stories is an integral part of the experience. Only make sure that all your guests stay with you, and that nobody gets too carried away with the stories. In Irving's tale, Ichabod Crane meets the very same Headless Horseman that he has heard about on the way home, and is never seen again. Was he embarrassed into leaving the town for good, or was he really carried off into the spirit world? Only we can tell, but just to be on the safe side, make sure there are no rivals in love at the banquet.

*"There was the doughty doughnut,
the tender olykoek, and the crisp
and crumbling cruller; sweet cakes and shortcakes,
ginger cakes and honey cakes, and the
whole family of cakes. And then there were
apple pies and peach pies and pumpkin pies;
besides slices of ham and smoked beef; and moreover
delectable dishes of preserved plums, and peaches,
and pears, and quinces; not to mention broiled
shad and roasted chickens; together with
bowls of milk and cream, all mingled
higgledy-piggledy, pretty much as I have
enumerated them, with the motherly teapot
sending up its clouds of vapor from the midst—
Heaven bless the mark!"*

Pendennis

William Makepeace Thackeray's novel *Pendennis* (1849–50) concerns the education of a lazy young man-about-town and his various amours. It was published in weekly installments at the same time as Dickens's classic *David Copperfield*, and both writers realized they were competing from then on to be the greatest in the public's mind. In the middle of writing *Pendennis*, a very autobiographical novel, Thackeray was struck down with fever—probably cholera—so the moment he recovered, Arthur Pendennis had to be struck down with fever too. On the other hand, the novel's bizarre chef Alcide Mirobolant does not seem to be taken from life at all. Nor does the extraordinary meal he cooks in order to seduce the vulgar but wealthy Blanche Amory.

YOU WILL NEED

- A DISTINGUISHED, IF LASCIVIOUS, CHEF
- SWEETBREADS, CHICKEN, AND PLOVERS' EGGS
- A BASKET OF APRICOT CAKE
- PLOMBIÈRE AND CHERRIES SHAPED AS INTERLOCKING HEARTS
- A LITTLE ROAST LAMB

~ À la Carte Blanche ~

Mirobolant, formerly the chef to the Duc de Borodino and Cardinal Beccfico, conceives a passion for Blanche and decides to inform her of this by serving a dinner that can leave her in no doubt at all of his feelings. He collects information about her favorite dishes, waits until her parents have gone out and she is entertaining a few friends, and begins the assault by cuisine. This opens with a dish inspired by Blanche's own name. As Mirobolant says, describing the meal to Madame Fribsbi: "Cupid is the father of invention."

"At her accustomed hour, instead of the rude gigot à l'eau which was ordinarily served at her too simple table, I sent her up a little potage à la Reine—à la Reine Blanche I called it—as white as her own tint—and confectioned with the most fragrant cream and almonds."

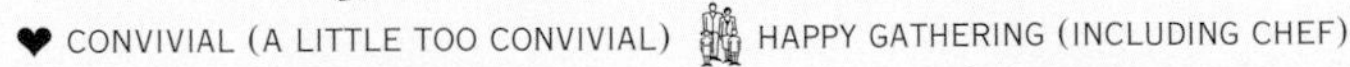

WELL-THUMBED CLASSIC · DELICIOUS

CONVIVIAL (A LITTLE TOO CONVIVIAL) · HAPPY GATHERING (INCLUDING CHEF)

~ PENDENNIS ROLE-PLAY ~

Mirobolant stands at the door of the dining room to watch Blanche's reaction to the feast, and to his delight hears her send her compliments to the chef—"we love him," says Blanche, convincing Mirobolant that he has succeeded in his chase. But since she is completely uncaring and wholly oblivious, the result is a series of misunderstandings that lead to an ugly brawl between Mirobolant and the eponymous hero. If you are doing this at home, there is really no need to repeat the duel, but you should note that the courses are very particular.

1) APPETIZER

The soup, *Potage à la Reine Blanche* (chicken soup with rice and vegetables) with added almonds and cream. If Mirobolant could have thought of other white food, he probably would have included that too, but be careful since semolina is unlikely to make the right impression.

2) INTERMEDIATE DISH

Filet de Merlan à l'Agnes (white fish with butter)—together with an *Eperlan à la Sainte Thérèse* (a kind of salmon). This course might perhaps be dropped depending on the size of the stomachs you are serving.

3) ENTRÉE

Sweetbreads and chicken, and a small roast lamb, laid on a bed of spinach, surrounded by pastry *croustillon*—representing sheep—and decorated by daisies and what Mirobolant calls "other savage flowers."

4) DESSERT

This is pudding *à la Reine Elisabeth* (a bread and milk mixture with butter, marshmallows, bananas, and raisins) and a dish of plovers' eggs called *Nid de Tourtereaux à la Roucoulez*, plus two flying birds touching beaks, a small apricot cake, and a marasquin jelly called *Ambroise de Calypso à la Souveraine de mon Coeur*.

5) LA PIÈCE DE RÉSISTANCE

Ice made of *plombière* and cherries shaped like two interconnected hearts. How could a girl resist?

"How do you think I had shaped them, Madame Fribsbi? In the form of two hearts united with an arrow, on which I had laid, before it entered, a bridal veil in cut paper, surmounted by a wreath of virginal orange-flowers."

Moby Dick

Few appreciated the merits of Herman Melville's classic *Moby Dick*—the story of one man's obsessive hunt for the Great White Whale—when it was published in 1851, or for many years afterward. Never mind that he had himself sailed on a whaler, though he jumped ship to join the U.S. Navy in the middle of the voyage. Never mind that Captain Ahab's bizarre obsession with his White Whale inspired the character of Captain Hook in *Peter Pan*. Never mind that the book has one of the most evocative chowder dinners (possibly the only chowder dinner) in the whole of literature. Melville still spent much of the next two decades as a customs officer in New York, and the merits of his novel remained unrecognized for years after his death. It is worth revisiting, if only because you are seeking inspiration for a seafood meal. Hosea Hussey's Try Pots Hotel in Nantucket serves an amazing chowder.

YOU WILL NEED

- GREAT BLACK COOKING POTS HUNG IN THE SHAPE OF A GALLOWS
- AN EXTREMELY DIRTY TABLECLOTH
- A LIMITED MENU: JUST CLAM OR COD
- BISCUITS AND PORK TO ADD FLAVOR
- A BAD-TEMPERED HOSTESS AT THE DOOR BAWLING AT THE OTHER GUESTS (HER YELLOW DRESS IS OPTIONAL)

~ COD OR CLAM? ~

The only choice offered by the landlady of Try Pots is "clam or cod?" Ishmael and the mysterious native American harpoonist Queeqeg—who is about to tell him the story of Ahab and Moby Dick—are recommended to try the hotel, and sit at a table with the leftovers from somebody else's meal. They expect little after a "cold and clammy reception." But when the meal arrives, it is a different story.

"Oh! Sweet friends, hearken to me.
It was made of small juicy clams,
scarcely bigger than hazel nuts,
mixed with pounded ship biscuit,
and salted pork cut up into little flakes;
the whole enriched with butter,
and plentifully seasoned with pepper and salt...
the chowder being surpassingly excellent,
we despatched it with great expedition."

WELL-THUMBED CLASSIC DELICIOUS
CONVIVIAL (BUT SMELLY)  TÊTE À TÊTE

~ MOBY DICK ROLE-PLAY ~

One of the peculiar aspects of the Try Pots Hotel is that almost everything there has something to do with fish. Chowder is the only item on the menu. Mrs. Hussey, the landlady, wears a necklace of cod vertebrae, and even the account books of the establishment are bound in shark skin. This is not the inspiration for a feast for someone who is allergic to seafood. But if you do try the *Moby Dick* meal, it is worth remembering three important rules to make the whole experience authentic.

1) THE MEAL HAS TO BE DIFFICULT TO FIND

Ishmael and Queeqeg have been given extraordinarily complex instructions for finding the Try Pots Hotel, and their memories of the exact location conflict. At the very least they have to knock on some local front doors and wake people up to work out where the place is. Try inviting your guests to your house and arranging the dinner at someone else's.

"A warm savory steam from the kitchen served to belie the apparently cheerless prospect before us…"

2) EVERYTHING HAS TO TASTE OF FISH

Almost everything at the Try Pots relates to fish in some way, and chowder is the only thing on the menu. Nantucket is one of those places that is absolutely drenched in the sea and seafaring, and even the milk tastes of fish. A sardine left in the bottom of the pitcher should do it.

"There was a fishy flavor to the milk too, which I could not at all account for, until one morning happening to take a stroll along the beach among some fisherman's boats, I saw Hosea's brindled cow feeding on the fish remains."

3) ABSOLUTELY NO HARPOONS

The one absolute rule of Mr. and Mrs. Hussey's household is that there should be no harpoons in the bedroom—even though every true whaleman sleeps with his harpoon—ever since one young man was found the next morning with his harpoon in his side. This detail should not be too difficult to achieve.

"So Mr Queeqeg… I will just take this here iron, and keep it for you till morning. But the chowder; clam or cod to-morrow for breakfast, men?"

Madame Bovary

GUSTAVE FLAUBERT'S novel *Madame Bovary* (1857) earned the young writer and his publisher an immediate prosecution for indecency. He was acquitted, but the cloud hung over him and his work for the rest of his life. Even so, his story about the terrible fate of a disillusioned provincial doctor's wife tempted by the high life, and her descent into debt and ruin, remains one of the pre-eminent French novels of all time. It is also linked to the emerging Impressionist art movement by its fascination for realism. So it should not be surprising that, when the Bovarys go out to dinner with the local marquis, every detail is recorded.

A WHIFF OF TRUFFLES

The splendidly lavish dinner, in the company of her rather dull husband, is a critical moment in Emma's awakening. She gets a glimpse at the table, weighed down with lobsters, candelabras, and silver dish covers, and it is a vision of the elegant sophisticated life she always dreamed about but that seems likely to elude her. Perhaps the iced champagne, served by an unsmiling steward in knee-britches, which made her shiver all over when she put it in her mouth, is to be the first step in her downfall. Once again we see how the stimulation of one appetite leads to the awakening of another.

YOU WILL NEED

- A SMALL ARMY OF STEWARDS
- A MARQUIS AND MARCHIONESS
- CANDLELIGHT REFLECTING IN SILVER DISH COVERS
- COOKED QUAILS IN THEIR FEATHERS
- PLATES OF CARVED ROAST MEATS
- ICED CHAMPAGNE AND POWDERED SUGAR
- THE FORMER LOVER OF MARIE ANTOINETTE

"Emma, on entering, felt herself wrapped round by the warm air, a blending of the perfume of flowers and of the fine linen, of the fumes of the viands, and the odor of the truffles."

WELL-THUMBED CLASSIC DELICIOUS
CONVIVIAL BANQUET

Flaubert was good enough to provide several important details about this meal for the purposes of reproduction. We know, for example, that it started at exactly 7 P.M. and that there was a ball afterward. We also know that the men sat on one table and the women on the other, which puts a potential damper on the evening. However, they would soon be swirling each other around the dance floor, which is more promising. We know what the room felt like to enter, with its warm smell of linen and truffles mixed with roasting meat and flowers, and the sight of the bread rolls on top of each napkin, folded on each plate like a bishop's miter. The following elements are also crucial.

1) DOUR-LOOKING STEWARDS

These are a vital part of the experience, wearing silk stockings, knee-britches, a white cravat, and frilled shirt. It is vital also that they absolutely never smile.

*"Smoke was rising; and in silk stockings,
knee-breeches, white cravat, and frilled shirt,
the steward, grave as a judge, offering ready carved
dishes between the shoulders of the guests,
with a touch of the spoon gave you the piece chosen."*

2) NEW TASTES

For Emma Bovary, part of the terrifying nervousness of the whole evening—apart from the fear that her husband will embarrass her by dancing—was that she has never before tasted many of the foods on the table. But then that is also part of the charm.

"She had never seen pomegranates nor tasted pineapples. The powdered sugar even seemed to her whiter and finer than elsewhere."

3) EXOTIC GUESTS

The most exciting guest to Emma is the marquis's father-in-law, a former lover of Queen Marie Antoinette, a notorious gambler and a multiple eloper, who sits at one end of the table with gravy drooling out of his mouth, one servant beside him bellowing descriptions of the dishes in front of him into his ear. Any re-creation of the Madame Bovary meal requires a notorious guest along these lines.

"Emma's eyes turned involuntarily to this old man with hanging lips, as to something extraordinary. He had lived at court and slept in the bed of queens!"

Beowulf

ONLY one manuscript copy in Anglo-Saxon survives of the epic poem *Beowulf*, but nobody knows when it was actually written. It could have been the eighth century or possibly later. Either way, it recounts the extraordinary tale of the hero Beowulf and his encounter with a terrifying half-human lake-dwelling monster called Grendel, who menaces the local area. Beowulf kills Grendel, but just as he and his warriors are relaxing into yet another daylong feast, Grendel's mother rouses herself from the lake to wreak revenge. Undoubtedly, the poem was recited when the chieftains were feasting, and most of the action happens to a background of feasting too, so clearly the Anglo-Saxons had their priorities right.

YOU WILL NEED

- A GREAT HALL
- CHIEFTAINS, THANES, AND MINSTRELS
- SHIELDS ALONG THE WALLS
- ROAST MEAT FINGER-STYLE
- ALE-CUPS
- FURRY OUTFITS
- A HIDEOUS SLATHERING MONSTER FROM THE LAGOON

~ Flowing Ale-Cups ~

Not only are Beowulf and his thanes feasting while Grendel's mother plots her comeback, but it is clear that that she and her son have a reasonably fixed intention of feasting on the warriors. So although the poem could not be said to go into great detail about what they all ate—epic poetry did not generally extend to recipes—we can be sure that eating is central to the story.

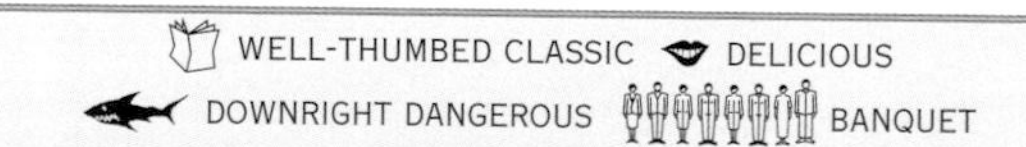

"Gathered together, the Geatish men
In the banquet-hall on bench assigned,
Sturdy-spirited, sat them down,
Hardy-hearted. A henchman attended,
Carried the carven cup in hand,
Served the clear mead.
Oft minstrels sang Blithe in Heorot."

GARGANTUA

FRANCOIS RABELAIS was a friar, a doctor, and one of the great satirical writers of all time. *Gargantua* (1535) is an obscure glimpse at episodes in the life and education of a relatively gentle giant. In fact, the five books in the cycle about the giant Gargantua and his son Pantagruel were banned by the Sorbonne, the French Parliament, and the Roman Catholic Church. Rabelais narrowly avoided prosecution for heresy. *Gargantua* in particular is packed with his love of food, drink, and excess, and his obsession with bodily functions. Most of the books leap from feasting to the great hunt for the perfect toilet paper (a goose's neck, he decides), and back to feasting again.

YOU WILL NEED

- AN ABSOLUTELY GARGANTUAN APPETITE
- 11 WILD BOAR, 303 BUZZARDS, AND OTHER ASSORTED MEAT AND GAME
- AN EXTREMELY LARGE FIRE
- A MASSIVE STAFF OF COOKS
- VERY SOFT TOILET PAPER (OR GOOSE IF NOT AVAILABLE)

THE WHOLE NINE YARDS

"I drink no more than a sponge," said Rabelais, but his creation, the vast Gargantua, has a rather larger appetite. In fact, some independent commentators might suggest a note of greed. One of his feasts alone includes 16 oxen, 6,000 pullets, and 300 pigs cooked in sweet wine. There is a certain grandeur about this kind of eating, and some of it is inherited by Gargantua's son, introduced in an earlier book.

WELL-THUMBED CLASSIC · DELICIOUS · CONVIVIAL
BANQUET (A ONE-PERSON FEAST)

"Without doubt there was meat enough, and it was handsomely dressed by Snapsauce, Hotchpot, and Brayverjuice, Grangousier's cooks. Jenkin Trudgeapace and Cleanglass were very careful to fill them drink."

~ GARGANTUA ROLE-PLAY ~

Gargantua's meals fall into the category of those it may be best not to repeat too precisely, for fear of bankruptcy. However, a loose reading of the text might give you a few ideas.

A LIGHT SALAD

When he felt the need of a salad, Gargantua simply reached for the whole field. Unfortunately on this occasion, the cabbages and lettuces conceal six pilgrims who are hiding there and who get eaten as well.

PANTAGRUEL'S PEARS

On another occasion, when served pears as part of a larger meal, Pantagruel asks what they are. This is the kind of surprise by exotic fruit that can go down well with guests.

"I like their taste extremely, said Pantagruel. If they were sliced, and put into a pan on the fire with wine and sugar, I fancy they would be very wholesome meat for the sick, as well as for the healthy. Pray what do you call 'em?"

THE GARGANTUA MEAL

No description of Gargantua's culinary inspiration would be complete without the menu for his banquet. Read and inwardly digest, if you dare.

"Besides his daily fare, were roasted sixteen oxen, three heifers, two and thirty calves, three score and three fat kids, four score and fifteen wethers, three hundred farrow pigs or sheats soused in sweet wine or must, eleven score partridges, seven hundred snipes and woodcocks, four hundred Loudun and Cornwall capons, six thousand pullets, and as many pigeons, six hundred crammed hens, fourteen hundred leverets, or young hares and rabbits, three hundred and three buzzards, and one thousand and seven hundred cockerels. For venison, they could not so suddenly come by it, only eleven wild boars, which the Abbot of Turpenay sent, and eighteen fallow deer which the Lord of Gramount bestowed; together with seven score pheasants, which were sent by the Lord of Essars; and some dozens of queests, coushats, ringdoves, and woodculvers; river-fowl, teals and awteals, bitterns, courtes, plovers, francolins, briganders, tyrasons, young lapwings, tame ducks, shovellers, woodlanders, herons, moorhens, criels, storks, canepetiers, oranges, flamans, which are phaenicopters, or crimson-winged sea-fowls, terrigoles, turkeys, arbens, coots, solan-geese, curlews, termagants, and water-wagtails, with a great deal of cream, curds, and fresh cheese, and store of soup, pottages, and brewis with great variety."

A Woman's Kingdom

Anton Pavlovich Chekhov, the great nineteenth-century playwright, trained as a doctor before giving it all up to be a full-time writer. He wrote vast numbers of short stories, and one of them—*A Woman's Kingdom* (1894), about a wealthy woman cut off from her former worker friends—has a particularly evocative family dinner. So if the idea of a sophisticated Russian dinner on Christmas Eve appeals, then this is the one to prepare. We are led to understand that it is far too good for the guest, Anna Akimovna's untrustworthy lawyer Lysevitch, who ends the meal by demanding a Christmas tip.

~ Oysters and Crayfish ~

A Woman's Kingdom features a very successful and powerful but lonely woman, Anna Akimovna, and we learn about two separate meals—one for the family (cabbage soup and suckling pig) and one French-style for visitors. This French dinner so excites Lysevitch that he starts eating it in his imagination, Pavlov-style, the moment he hears the clatter of crockery. But Lysevitch is a model we should be careful not to copy when we re-create the Chekhov meal: he munches loudly, with the most disgusting noises emerging from his nose.

YOU WILL NEED

- AN OPEN FIRE
- CABBAGE SOUP, PIG, TURBOTS, AND MUCH ELSE BESIDES
- PERFECT WINES
- LITERARY CONVERSATION
- CIGARS
- COFFEE AND LIQUEURS
- PADDED WAISTCOATS
- FAKE MUSTACHES

FAMILY MEAL:

Cabbage Soup, Suckling Pig, Goose with Apples

FRENCH MEAL:

Matelote of Turbots,

Fresh White Mushrooms in Cream,

Oyster and Crayfish Sauce

LATER: *Salt Meat*

TO DRINK: *French wine*

 A GOOD READ  DELICIOUS  CONVIVIAL  HAPPY GATHERING

EATING OUTDOORS

MACBETH

WELCOME to the most famous recipe in literature, set out in gory detail by the three witches that Macbeth consults about his destiny in an unpleasant cavern on a blasted heath. In fact, the recipe is so precise— "eye of newt and toe of frog," for example—that it has given rise to rumors over the centuries that this was a real witches' spell that William Shakespeare was using. The rumor is one of the main reasons why his most famous tragedy is considered so unlucky. Anyone wanting to serve this concoction in their own home should bear another crucial consideration in mind: there is no record in the play of the witches actually eating it.

YOU WILL NEED

- A BLASTED HEATH
- A CAULDRON
- MATCHES OR A LIGHTER
- ACCESS TO THE LABORATORY OF A RETIRED ALCHEMIST
- NOSE OF TURK
- TARTAR'S LIPS
- ESCARGOTS AND FROG LEGS IF YOU CAN'T FIND THE ABOVE

~ HUBBLE AND BUBBLE ~

If you are still keen to try this at home, there is another major problem. Some of the ingredients are rare: the finger of birth-strangled babe is hard to get hold of these days. So is the sweat from the murderer's gibbet. The tooth of wolf might possibly be available, but the scale of dragon is downright mythical. Snails, frog legs, and snakemeat make good substitutes.

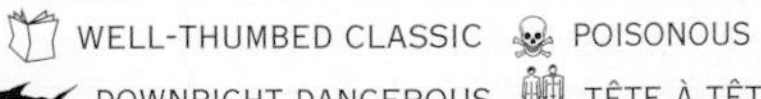

WELL-THUMBED CLASSIC  POISONOUS

DOWNRIGHT DANGEROUS  TÊTE À TÊTE

~ MACBETH ROLE-PLAY ~

Shakespeare's drama of his famous Scottish lord who usurps the throne of Scotland was probably written in 1606, just as England was getting used to having its own Scottish king on the throne. The scene when Macbeth consults the witches allows us to watch the recipe taking shape ingredient by ingredient, but leaves us with some confusion about which one is crucial—is this Tongue of Dog Pudding or Sow's Blood Soup, for example? There are also three aspects of the whole affair that mark the picnic out as unique:

1) TIMELY INGREDIENTS

Many of the ingredients are not just in there for the taste, but for their magical effects—and that means something extra. This is not just "slips of yew," for example, but yew that has been "silver'd in the moon's eclipse." So be careful.

2) DUBIOUS INTENTIONS

You can't be certain, of course, but there is some question about the hosts' goodwill here. No wonder they refer to the recipe as "a deed without a name."

"By the pricking of my thumbs,
Something wicked this way comes."

3) MODE OF ADDRESSING HOST

However mixed your feelings for your hosts might be at any given meal, it is probably best not to address them as Macbeth does in this case. "How now, you secret, black and midnight hags," is not a form of address likely to lead to a repeat invitation.

"Fillet of a fenny snake,
In the cauldron boil and bake;
Eye of newt and toe of frog,
Wool of bat and tongue of dog,
Adder's fork and blind-worm's sting,
Lizard's leg and owlet's wing,
For a charm of powerful trouble,
Like a hell-broth boil and bubble."

The Walrus and the Carpenter

THERE is no need to be a vegetarian to perceive a hidden cruelty at the heart of your average dinner. Most people prefer not to think of it, but Mary's Little Lamb can all too often become tonight's ragout. Writing rather brutal nonsense for children, Lewis Carroll was able to pinpoint exactly this uneasiness in a couple of rhymes in his sequel to *Alice's Adventures in Wonderland*, which he called *Through the Looking Glass* (1871). There is the mock turtle weeping over the soup, but most disturbingly, there are the Walrus and the Carpenter inviting all the little oysters to dinner, and then gobbling them up. It is, as the oysters remark, "a dismal thing to do."

YOU WILL NEED

- A SMALL ARMY OF PLUMP, YOUTHFUL OYSTERS IN NEED OF A CHAT
- BREAD SPREAD THICKLY WITH BUTTER
- A BEACH
- PEPPER AND VINEGAR
- SOME SILLY QUESTIONS (E.G., IS THE SEA BOILING HOT?)
- A SARDONIC ATTITUDE

ANSWER CAME THERE NONE

There is some confusion over which meal we are talking about here, since the sun was shining on the sea, although Carroll remarks helpfully that it was the middle of the night. What is certain is that the Walrus and the Carpenter persuade the poor little oysters to come for a walk with them before the meal. Afterward the Walrus sheds a few tears, but the Carpenter just complains that his butter is spread too thickly. Who are they? Critics claim that they represent nineteenth-century British Prime Ministers Gladstone and Disraeli, even Jesus Christ and the Buddha. In fact, Carroll seems to have chosen them because the words "walrus and carpenter" scanned nicely. He even told his illustrator he could choose to draw a baronet or a butterfly.

" 'A loaf of bread,' the Walrus said,
'Is what we chiefly need:
Pepper and vinegar besides
Are very good indeed—
Now if you're ready, Oysters dear,
We can begin to feed.' "

EMMA

EMMA is the last and greatest of Jane Austen's novels (1816), published the year before she died at the age of only forty-one. It has been adapted, modernized, and filmed countless times, and tells the complicated story of the heroine's attempts to marry off her friend Harriet, and her slow realization of who she herself really loves. Can you write a whole novel about that? Well, yes. Austen manages because of her extraordinary characters and razor-sharp wit. But there has to be a backdrop to the slowly unfolding plot, and this is made up of the succession of sociable meals where Emma, Harriet, Mr. Knightley, Miss Bates, and the raucous Mrs. Elton meet so regularly. And most of these occasions are picnics.

YOU WILL NEED

- A MEDIEVAL ABBEY CONVERTED MANY CENTURIES AGO INTO A COUNTRY HOUSE
- GREEN FIELDS, HILLS, AND SHEEP IN THE DISTANCE
- BASKETS AND BONNETS
- STRAWBERRIES
- MORE STRAWBERRIES
- GOSSIP

~ ONLY STRAWBERRIES SPOKEN OF ~

Of all the picnics among the elite of Highbury, the strawberry-picking picnic at Donwell Abbey stands out from them all. The party wanders along the strawberry beds at the abbey picking the best ones they can find, eating or collecting them in baskets, and gossiping about each other. There is only one thing on the menu, but in that beautiful, green, rural scene, it seems to be enough. The great advantage of this feast is that there is no cooking and no cleanup.

"Mrs Elton, in all her apparatus of happiness, her large bonnet and her basket, was very ready to lead the way in gathering, accepting, or talking—strawberries, and only strawberries, could now be thought or spoken of—'The best fruit in England—everybody's favourite—always wholesome.'"

UNPUTDOWNABLE DELICIOUS CONVIVIAL HAPPY GATHERING

~ EMMA ROLE-PLAY ~

For someone who spent almost her entire literary career writing about meals, parties, dancing, and picnics, Jane Austen describes food remarkably little. Maybe the food is beside the point. She was, after all, writing during an age of middle-class over-eating, so maybe her characters take it all for granted. Even so, if you are seeking inspiration in *Emma*, there are quite a number of meals to choose from, even if you sometimes have to use your imagination to fill in some of the gaps in the menu. As well as the strawberry picnic at Donwell Abbey, you will also need to try the following.

1) SUPPER WITH THE WOODHOUSES

Emma's own entertainment for the ladies of Highbury is complicated by the presence of her hypochondriacal father, who believes that almost any supper is extremely bad for the digestion, and says so as the guests tuck in.

> *"One of our small eggs will not hurt you. Miss Bates, let Emma help you to a little bit of tart—a very little bit. Ours are all apple-tarts. You need not be afraid of unwholesome preserves here. I do not advise the custard. Mrs. Goddard, what say you to half a glass of wine? A small half-glass, put into a tumbler of water? I do not think it could disagree with you."*

2) DINNER WITH THE WESTONS

It is a truth universally acknowledged that when you have any kind of entertainment, the guests must be in want of dinner. The Westons' party, which begins with just sandwiches on the menu, soon expands into something more splendid.

"The baked apples and biscuits, excellent in their way, you know; but there was a delicate fricassee of sweetbread and some asparagus brought in at first, and good Mr. Woodhouse, not thinking the asparagus quite boiled enough, sent it all out again."

Goblin Market

Literature and folklore are full of the most explicit warnings about what you should do and not do when you run into fairies. *Goblin Market* (1862), Christina Rossetti's most successful poem, fits the bill, describing the rescue of one sister by another from the lure of the goblin fruits. The sister of the artist Dante Gabriel Rossetti and a one-person literary wing of the Pre-Raphaelite Brotherhood, she shared their fascination with medieval legend, and their taste for high Episcopalian religion. But she may have been frustrated that—according to critics—she never quite surpassed *Goblin Market*. Instead she turned to religious poems for children.

YOU WILL NEED

- A VERY GREAT DEAL OF FRUIT
- A NUMBER OF LASCIVIOUS GOBLINS
- A SISTER (OR FRIEND) WHO CAN RESCUE YOU IF THINGS GO WRONG

~ FORBIDDEN FRUITS ~

The eating by Lizzie and Laura of the fruits offered so temptingly by the goblin men is so illicit that this is only arguably a picnic. Certainly there is no sitting down to a congenial meal—more like a frenzied gorging on fruit juice. So much so that feminist critics ever since have discussed exactly what it means—do the goblin fruits stand for sex or lust, or maybe a kind of lesbianism? But perhaps Rossetti is simply writing a conventional warning—against eating between meals.

A GOOD READ · DELICIOUS · DOWNRIGHT DANGEROUS
TÊTE À TÊTE (PLUS GOBLINS)

"Come buy our orchard fruits,
Come buy, come buy: Apples and quinces,
Lemons and oranges, Plump unpecked cherries—
Melons and raspberries, Bloom-down-cheeked peaches,
Swart-headed mulberries, Wild free-born cranberries,
Crab-apples, dewberries, Pine-apples, blackberries,
Apricots, strawberries—All ripe together
In summer weather."

Three Men in a Boat

ONE of the comic masterpieces of the past century and a half, *Three Men in a Boat* (1888–89) made the name and career of the author Jerome K. Jerome overnight. It also made boating up the River Thames from London extremely fashionable. By the year after it was published there were as many as 12,000 boats for hire on the river.

Jerome was also an exponent of what was known as the "New Journalism"—an early version of human interest feature-writing—and the story of his trip up the river with George and Harris, and the dog Montmorency, was based on real excursions he made with the real versions of the fictional friends. Only the dog was completely imaginary. And just as meals dominate the mind when you are on a weeklong excursion by small boat, so they dominate the action in the book.

YOU WILL NEED

- A BOAT
- TWO FRIENDS AND A DOG
- A SMALL STOVE
- COLD PIE
- A TENT THAT NOBODY HAS SUCCESSFULLY ERECTED BEFORE
- CHEESE AND METHYLATED SPIRITS WITH EVERYTHING
- MILD HYPOCHONDRIA

~ NOT TO MENTION THE DOG ~

The picnics in the boat shared by the Three Men are hit-and-miss affairs. They tend to leave eating till the afternoon has gone and the evening has continued on into night, while they get on with the rowing, or spend some hours trying to put up the tent. These makeshift suppers are often extremely satisfying as the day's accumulated hunger pangs are assuaged. Sometimes, on the other hand, they are damp and depressing, and even the dog rejects the leftovers.

"Everything in the boat was damp and clammy. Supper was not a success. Cold veal pie, when you don't feel hungry, is apt to cloy. I felt I wanted whitebait and a cutlet; Harris babbled of soles and white-sauce, and passed the remains of his pie to Montmorency, who declined it, and, apparently insulted by the offer, went and sat over at the other end of the boat by himself."

UNPUTDOWNABLE · BARELY EDIBLE · CONVIVIAL
HAPPY GATHERING (INCLUDING DOG)

~ THREE MEN IN A BOAT ROLE-PLAY ~

The main purpose behind the trip taken up the Thames by the narrator, George, Harris, and Montmorency is health. All three are dramatic hypochondriacs, but a good meal—when they achieve it—makes a very big difference to their mood. The difficulty is that it usually involves boiling the kettle at the end of the boat which, like every watched pot, never boils if anyone is so much as thinking about it. Only when they proclaim how little they want hot water does the kettle achieve its objective and put out the stove. The *Three Men in a Boat* meal can take inspiration from either of the following.

I) THE LAST SUPPER

This supper is served at their lodgings before the trio set out, but is put before them during a comparison of their medical symptoms. This puts them horribly off the meal—though there is no reason why you should not enjoy their steak, onions, and rhubarb tart.

> *"We smiled sadly at one another, and said we supposed we had better try to swallow a bit. Harris said a little something in one's stomach often kept the disease in check; and Mrs. Poppets brought the tray in, and we drew up to the table, and toyed with a little steak and onions, and some rhubarb tart."*

2) THE WET PICNIC

The main experience of eating in the boat is that it is a damp business. The food is damp, the tobacco is damp, and the methylated spirit stove has trouble heating or drying anything very much. If you can't wait for it to rain, the same effect can be achieved by leaving the lawn sprinkler on while you eat, or else by holding your picnic in the bathtub or shower.

"Rainwater is the chief article of diet at supper. The bread is two-thirds rainwater, the beefsteak-pie is exceedingly rich in it, and the jam, and the butter, and the salt, and the coffee have all combined with it to make soup."

CHILDREN'S MEALS

THE WIND IN THE WILLOWS

THE great English love affair with boats and boating has produced a wealth of fine literature and nothing finer than Kenneth Grahame's classic children's story *The Wind in the Willows* (1908). The author was a reluctant banker, who wrote most of the original story in letters to his son Alistair, and never intended for it to be published. Fortunately for us, he was persuaded to offer the adventures of Mole, Badger, Water Rat, and the impossible Toad to a wider public, and the rest, as they say, is history.

~ TALES OF THE RIVER BANK ~

The book describes the sad decline of Mr. Toad and the loss of his home—and its dramatic recapture—to wild woodland creatures like weasels, ferrets, and stoats. But it begins with a picnic by the river bank. This is organized by the Water Rat, who invites his new friend the Mole, and they are joined shortly afterward by the Badger, and a passing otter. The passage where Rat indexes the contents of the picnic basket to his friend is one of the most famous shopping lists in literature.

YOU WILL NEED

- A VERY LARGE PICNIC HAMPER
- A SELECTION OF COLD MEATS
- SANDWICHES
- GINGER BEER AND LEMONADE
- A PLEASANT RIVERSIDE SPOT
- A SMALL BOAT
- A BIG TABLECLOTH

"'There's cold chicken inside it,' replied the Rat briefly; 'coldtonguecoldhamcoldbeefpickledgherkinssaladfrenchrolls cresssandwichespottedmeatgingerbeerlemonadesodawater—' 'O stop, stop,' cried the Mole in ecstasies: 'This is too much!' 'Do you really think so?' enquired the Rat seriously. 'It's only what I always take on these little excursions; and the other animals are always telling me that I'm a mean beast and cut it VERY fine!'"

A GOOD READ DELICIOUS CONVIVIAL HAPPY GATHERING

~ WIND IN THE WILLOWS ROLE-PLAY ~

There are some hearty breakfasts in *The Wind in the Willows*— but why are there also so many rushed and impromptu meals? Well, obviously because the characters are engaged in a struggle to seize back Toad Hall from the creatures of the Wild Wood, and when you are campaigning—as any soldier or politician will tell you—you must make do with what is at hand. Following the *Wind in the Willows* eating regime therefore requires you to raid the pantry at random to see if there is anything there. You may find the following useful:

1) BE PREPARED

Actually, there seems to be very little impromptu about the Water Rat's picnic. As a nautical kind of person, the Rat prefers to be led where the whimsy takes him, but the large basket suggests that he doesn't extend this happenstance attitude to matters of the stomach.

"His excited friend shook out the table-cloth and spread it, took out all the mysterious packets one by one and arranged their contents in due order, still gasping, 'O my! O my!' at each fresh revelation."

2) BADGER'S BREAKFAST

To reproduce the Badger's breakfast, you really need a troupe of trained hedgehogs, for it is these creatures that do the cooking and serve the food. The main item on the menu is fried ham, but if you can't get any hedgehog chefs, you could always have it cold instead.

"'Rather!' replied the Otter, winking at the Mole. 'The sight of these greedy young hedgehogs stuffing themselves with fried ham makes me feel positively famished.'"

3) SARDINES

Mole invites Ratty back to his neglected home, Mole End, and bitterly regrets doing so when he sees the layers of dust over all the furniture. There is apparently nothing to eat except what bits and pieces can be found in the cupboards.

"They went and foraged accordingly, hunting through every cupboard and turning out every drawer. The result was not so very depressing after all, though of course it might have been better; a tin of sardines—a box of captain's biscuits, nearly full—and a German sausage encased in silver paper."

Oliver Twist

THREE years before Charles Dickens published *Oliver Twist* (1837), the British government had swept away the old Poor Law—which provided for paupers to be given money for food by their local parish—and replaced it with a network of workhouses. By the time Dickens was writing about the motherless Oliver, he was incensed at the abuses in these new centers. The brutal conditions were also becoming public news: husbands separated from wives, demeaning uniforms, and a diet calculated to keep the inmates alive without attracting anyone to the idea of living there. And so the scene is set for the orphan Oliver Twist to be chosen by lot by his fellows to go up to the workhouse overseer after supper, and ask for some more.

YOU WILL NEED

- A LARGE CAULDRON AND SERVING SPOON
- A MEAGER QUANTITY OF GRUEL
- AN ONION (ON THE RIGHT DAY)
- AN APRON
- A BUSLOAD OF RAGGED, HUNGRY BOYS
- A SERIOUS DOSE OF HYPOCRISY

~ FOOD, GLORIOUS FOOD ~

Oliver and his colleagues have been unnerved by the threat of one of the taller boys that, being so hungry, he might be forced to eat the boy who slept next to him. Not surprising, since all they are given is three meals of thin gruel a day, eked out with oatmeal, served by the master dressed in an apron with a large serving spoon, with an onion twice a week and half a roll on Sundays. Oliver's request, bowl in hand, is greeted with horror by the master, and by the Poor Law Guardians who run the establishment, and he finds himself expelled and sold to the highest bidder among the local tradespeople.

"The bowls never wanted washing. The boys polished them with their spoons till they shone again; and when they had performed this operation (which never took very long, the spoons being nearly as large as the bowls), they would sit staring at the copper, with such eager eyes, as if they could have devoured the very bricks of which it was composed."

UNPUTDOWNABLE · BARELY EDIBLE

LONELY (IN SOCIAL KIND OF WAY)

BANQUET (BUT BRING SUPPLEMENTS)

~ OLIVER TWIST ROLE-PLAY ~

Oliver Twist was Dickens's first runaway success, with its colorful characters—Mr Bumble the Beadle, Fagin, Bill Sikes, and his dog—giving the audience a taste, not just of gruel, but of the London underworld. Still it's not all gruel, and there are some meals that might be worth trying out.

1) MR. BUMBLE'S MEAL

The fat and hypocritical beadle, the parish overseer of the poor, plays a continuing role in the story as one of those who discover Oliver's real identity. During his regular meal at a coaching inn, he comes upon a reminder of Oliver's existence in the form of a newspaper advertisement. Steak, oyster sauce, and porter should give you plenty of energy for oppressing the poor of the parish, or your local equivalent.

"Having disposed of these evil-minded persons for the night, Mr Bumble sat himself down in the house at which the coach stopped; and took a temperate dinner of steaks, oyster sauce, and porter."

2) THE ARTFUL DODGER'S MEAL

Alone in the unfamiliar streets of London, Oliver encounters the skillful young pickpocket, the Artful Dodger, who treats him to a bang-up meal. You will need some beer to wash this one down.

"Assisting Oliver to rise, the young gentleman took him to an adjacent chandler's shop, where he purchased a sufficiency of ready-dressed ham and a half-quartern loaf, or, as he himself expressed it, 'a fourpenny bran!' the ham being kept clean and preserved from dust, by the ingenious expedient of making a hole in the loaf by pulling out a portion of the crumb, and stuffing it therein."

3) FAGIN'S MEAL

Brought home to Fagin's lair, with all the other trainee pickpockets, Oliver partakes in the meal that Fagin is cooking, toasting-fork in hand like the Devil himself. You will also need hot gin-and-water for this meal, which is used to put Oliver to sleep.

"There was a deal table before the fire: upon which were a candle, stuck in a ginger-beer bottle, two or three pewter pots, a loaf and butter, and a plate. In a frying-pan, which was on the fire, and which was secured to the mantelshelf by a string, some sausages were cooking."

The Adventures of Huckleberry Finn

ALTHOUGH we have categorized it as a children's book, Mark Twain's *The Adventures of Huckleberry Finn* (1884) is not only one of the best-loved works of American literature, but is now hailed as one of the greatest. It was billed as the sequel to his novel *Tom Sawyer*, but it has long since overtaken that in popularity. Even so, it is tough for a children's book—there is murder, alcoholism, and disturbing racism as Huck and the runaway slave Jim sail down the Mississippi on a makeshift raft. There is also a great deal to eat, though most of it has been stolen by Huckleberry Finn.

~ And Catfish Too ~

Huckleberry Finn struggles with the concept of slavery, nearly three decades after its abolition, and through their loyalty to each other, Huck and Jim are both recaptured and sent home—only to find the twist in the plot which will set Jim free. Huck Finn is one of those boys who can turn his hand to almost anything—and with a brutal, alcoholic father he has to live by his wits. Among his accomplishments, the combination of thieving and cookery skills seems to get him a long way. The meal he cooks for Jim shortly after meeting him is so astonishing that Jim believes it is done by witchcraft. Actually, it is simply a combination of bacon, coffee, and the catfish Huck has caught from the river and fried.

YOU WILL NEED

- CORNMEAL, BACON, CATFISH AND COFFEE
- A COFFEE POT AND SKILLET
- TIN CUPS AND SUGAR
- A SMALL BARBECUE
- A GRASSY SPOT NEXT TO ONE OF THE GREAT RIVERS ON EARTH
- CHECKERED SHIRTS

"When breakfast was ready we lolled on the grass and eat it smoking hot. Jim laid it in with all his might, for he was most about starved. Then when we had got pretty well stuffed, we laid off and lazied."

A GOOD READ DELICIOUS CONVIVIAL TÊTE À TÊTE

~ HUCKLEBERRY FINN ROLE-PLAY ~

Mark Twain—real name Samuel L. Clemens—was a journalist from Missouri who began his career on the Mississippi steamboats, made a fortune with *Huckleberry Finn* and his other novels, and lost it again in a financial crash. He always claimed *Huckleberry Finn* was just for fun, but at the same time it is a serious book and a serious look at American society. It also provides a number of possible inspirations for meals.

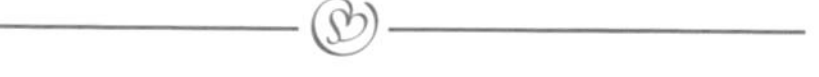

1) THE WIDOW DOUGLAS MEAL

There are drawbacks to this meal—it is simply all the Widow's leftovers mixed up together—and you also have to sweat in a hot room wearing too many clothes. For added authenticity, find an old lady to recite interminable Bible stories afterward.

"In a barrel of odds and ends it is different; things get mixed up, and the juice kind of swaps around, and the things go better."

2) THE PAP MEAL

Pap is Huck's brutal father, and although he does not actually eat this meal—he really only drinks—he does collect together the ingredients in a skiff, from where Huck removes it. Authenticity requires you to wait for a chance to sail this meal away before you can eat it, so it's good for excursions on the boating lake in the park.

"The old man made me go to the skiff and fetch the things he had got. There was a fifty-pound sack of corn meal, and a side of bacon, ammunition, and a four-gallon jug of whisky, and an old book and two newspapers for wadding, besides some tow."

3) THE JIM MEAL

Jim rescues Huck by raft from a murderous feud, and after hanging up the signal lamp as they sail down the Mississippi, Jim cooks one of the most successful meals in the book. It should be eaten on a raft, though you might have had enough of boats by now.

"I hadn't had a bite to eat since yesterday, so Jim he got out some corn-dodgers and buttermilk, and pork and cabbage and greens—there ain't nothing in the world so good when it's cooked right—and whilst I eat my supper we talked and had a good time."

Swallows and Amazons

There are a number of mysteries connected with the journalist Arthur Ransome, author of *Swallows and Amazons* (1930) and the other novels in the sequence about the adventures of a group of children in northern England's the Lake District. This is the beautiful region of lakes and mountains that so inspired the poet William Wordsworth, and it certainly inspired Ransome. One of the mysteries is the precise work that Ransome was doing in his earlier years in St. Petersburg. It seems that he was spying, but it has never been quite clear for whom—though he did marry Trotsky's secretary and bring her home to England to live in the Lake District.

YOU WILL NEED

- A LAKE AND SMALL DINGHY
- SCRAMBLED EGG WITH BROWN BREAD AND BUTTER
- MILK (BUT GO EASY BECAUSE THERE ISN'T ENOUGH FOR TOMORROW)
- RICE PUDDING, SEED CAKE, AND APPLES
- A KETTLE OF BOILING WATER ON A SMALL FIRE
- SHORT PANTS AND SENSIBLE SHOES

~ Scrambled Eggs and Toast ~

Swallow is the name of the little boat that the children use to sail away to a secluded bay, where they set up camp. The captain's mate and cook is Susan, and she wields the skillet. This is no mean feast—scrambled eggs plus tea and brown bread and butter, followed by rice pudding from a cookie tin and big slices of seed cake. In fact, this is one of the most comforting meals you will find in this whole book. If ever you find yourself marooned on an island with a small boat, then a meal of fried eggs, followed by cookies or cake will immediately cheer you.

INSTRUCTIONS

First melt the butter in a skillet
and empty in the raw eggs.
Stir together with pepper and salt.
Serve on thick slices of brown bread and butter.
Scrape the dishes, pan, and spoons in the lake.
Keep a sharp lookout with your telescope.

 A GOOD READ  DELICIOUS ❤ CONVIVIAL  HAPPY GATHERING

SPECIAL OCCASIONS

SAMUEL PEPYS'S DIARY

THERE really is nobody quite like Samuel Pepys, who was the secretary of the Royal Navy under both Cromwell and Charles II in seventeenth-century London. But between 1659 and 1669 he was also secretly keeping a meticulously honest account of his life in shorthand—so his wife would be unable to read it—which he was at pains to protect after his death. It was discovered a century later and finally published in 1825. In it we can follow his obsessions, his lusts, his rows with his wife, disastrous theater outings, frustrations at work, lewd encounters in the parks—and his meals.

YOU WILL NEED

- ROASTED MEAT (RABBIT, LAMB, BEEF, CHICKEN)
- PUDDINGS AND TARTS
- CHEESE
- OYSTERS
- MORE CHEESE
- A TABLE UNDER WHICH TO FONDLE THE LEGS OF GUESTS
- A LONG CURLY WIG

~ SUPPER AND SO TO BED ~

The diary is full of Pepys's meals, and even meals that he was excluded from—like the Duke of York's, the future James II, at Whitehall Palace, where Pepys waxes lyrical on the parsley sauce. In 1664 he buys a fork for the first time, and one of the first diary entries records that he has drunk a "cup of tee (a China drink) of which I never had drunk before."

"[The Duke of York] did mightily magnify his sauce which he did then eat with everything, and said it was the best universal sauce in the world... I by and by did taste it, and liked it mightily."

A GOOD READ DELICIOUS CONVIVIAL BANQUET

~ PEPYS ROLE-PLAY ~

Pepys betrays his priorities nowhere more than in his extraordinary account of the Great Fire of London in 1666, at the height of which he buries his most treasured possessions—gold, wine, and a great cheese—in his garden to escape the destruction. There is no doubt that if you are seeking inspiration for the Pepys meal, there is an extraordinary variety to choose from across the nine years of his diary—from the marrow bones and two dozen larks (24 January 1659) to the Duke of York's sauce a decade later (10 February 1669).

1) A PIECE OF CAKE

The Great Fire of London was preceded by the Great Plague in 1665. It might be stretching a point to suggest that this was a special occasion, but although thousands were dying all around him, Pepys had the time of his life. His wife was out of town for safety, and he took a trip with a girl he calls "the fairest flower" out to tea.

"I took coach and to Westminster Hall, where I took the fairest flower, and by coach to Tothill Fields for the ayre till it was dark. I 'light, and in with the fairest flower to eat a cake, and there did do as much as was safe with my flower, and that was enough on my part. Broke up, and away without any notice."

2) THE PEPYS MEAL

Entertaining his friends Dr. Clerke and Mr. Pierce and their wives and relations, Pepys manages to serve for them, after oysters as a first course, a hash of rabbits, a lamb, and a rare cut of beef. Plus the usual tart, fruit, and cheese, and then again cold meat at 10 P.M. before sending them home. It is a long day, but worth it.

"Next a great dish of roasted fowl, cost me about 30 shillings, and a tart, and then fruit and cheese. My dinner was noble and enough."

3) THE PENN MEAL

Pepys particularly dislikes Admiral Sir William Penn, who he believes spends all his money on elegant clothes and then is mean with his guests at the dinner table. This is a meal where you can have revenge on those you have invited.

"So to Sir W. Penn's, where my wife was, and supped with a little, but yet little mirth, and a bad, nasty supper, which makes me not love the family, they do all things so meanly, to make a little bad show upon their backs."

Mr. Sponge's Sporting Tour

Mr. Sponge and his friends, the heroes of R.S. Surtees's novel (1853), have always excited some snobbery among literary critics. They are hunting people without much interest in anything else, except possibly eating. Mr. Sponge himself manages to eke out a living by selling horses to people for more than they are worth. He is hardly an example of heroic stature. But for anyone in search of literary cuisine, there is a great deal of riotous eating in *Mr. Sponge's Sporting Tour*—most of it before, during, and after a hunt. These were the days before snacks, after all—though it is worth noting that 1853 was also the year when, quite by accident, the potato chip was invented.

A HUNTING MEAL

This is no romantic novel. It describes the travels of Mr. Sponge as he mooches off friends and acquaintances, and their adventures trying to encourage him to move on. The most evocative hunt meal is the late breakfast served by the farmer Mr. Springwheat, which gets out of hand. After eating "soup, game, tea, coffee, chocolate, eggs, honey, marmalade, crepes, pines, melons, buns," not to mention disposing of some cases of champagne, the guests at this entertainment fall back on eating the sugar table decorations. The only complication if you are re-creating this meal is the need to leave the table at any moment in pursuit of a fox.

YOU WILL NEED

- HOME-FRIED TURKEY
- A SIDEBOARD GROANING WITH MEAT
- CAKES, AND JELLIES WITHOUT END
- COFFEE AND CHAMPAGNE
- SUGAR TABLE DECORATIONS
- A HORSE AND HOUNDS IN THE YARD OUTSIDE
- CHERRY BRANDY

"'Well, but I s'pose we may as well fall to,' observed his lordship, casting his eye upon the well-garnished table. 'All these good things are meant to eat, I s'pose,' added he: 'cakes, and sweets, and jellies without end: and as to your sideboard,' said he, turning round and looking at it, 'it's a match for any Lord Mayor's. A round of beef, a ham, a tongue, and is that a goose or a turkey?'"

A GOOD READ DELICIOUS CONVIVIAL BANQUET

THE GREAT GATSBY

NONE of the American novels of the 1920s quite captured the spirit of the age like F. Scott Fitzgerald's *The Great Gatsby* (1925)—the pleasure-seeking, youthful, shallow gaiety of the period that ended with the Wall Street Crash in 1929. *The Great Gatsby* is not about food and drink, yet there it is in the background, from the splendor of Gatsby's famous receptions to the cold chicken on a plate as Tom and Daisy try to sort out the great holes emerging in their marriage.

~ BANJOS ON THE LAWN ~

This is a novel about a hedonistic America in the roaring twenties. It describes the narrator's slow disillusion with the wonderful Gatsby, as he realizes that he is eaten up with love for the wife of one of his guests, and—like the world he represents—is doomed to a rather shabby end. Gatsby himself is well known for the extraordinary parties that he throws at his luxurious Gothic mansion in West Egg, the less-fashionable side of Long Island. There are mysterious whisperings that he is not quite the genial host he seems, of bootlegging and the underworld, but then nothing in Gatsby's world is quite what it seems. The parties conceal a world-weariness that overcomes all of the characters. But before it does, don't pass up the opportunity presented by a true Gatsby meal. First, set the mood by tasting a Great Gatsby Cocktail, the Mint Julep.

YOU WILL NEED

- CHAMPAGNE AND CLARET
- WINE GLASSES BIGGER THAN FINGER BOWLS
- MOONLIGHT ON THE LAWN
- BANJO PLAYERS AND JAZZ SINGERS
- TWO SUPPERS, FIVE HOURS APART
- OLD MEN DANCING WITH YOUNG GIRLS
- AN AIR OF WORLD-WEARY SOPHISTICATION

MINT JULEP

Put some fresh mint sprigs in a bowl,
add a teaspoon of sugar and
a quarter of an ounce of water.
Crush the leaves with a spoon and stir it together.
Next, fill a tumbler with crushed ice
and bourbon whiskey and put the mixture
in a bowl on the top.
Add another layer of crushed ice,
and so on until you can't wait any longer.

~ GREAT GATSBY ROLE-PLAY ~

For a novel about greed and depravity, *The Great Gatsby* is surprisingly compelling in the elusive dream it manages to weave. Much as we might disapprove of the brutish Tom Buchanan and his racism and bullying; much as we might nod our heads at the inevitability of Gatsby's fall, there is some aspect of the whole thing that makes us want to grace the lawn in West Egg in the heady summer of 1922 and sip the champagne from the enormous glasses ourselves. It's a little like remembering our own youth, and all the more reason for throwing a *Great Gatsby*-style entertainment.

1) THE GATSBY PARTY

This involves moonlight on the lawn, banjo players, jazz singers, and what the narrator calls "old men pushing young girls backward in eternal graceless circles." The food is not specified, but the drink—at this event considerably more important—is described right down to the size of the glasses, which are bigger than finger bowls. It is certainly decadent, but it may still be worth a try, especially if you dress like Gatsby himself in a pink suit under the moon.

2) THE GATSBY LUNCH

This one is a little more casual. There is a "succulent hash" served to Gatsby and two companions in a cellar in New York's 42nd Street, but we have the uneasy feeling that all is not right with the place. A friend of one of the men was shot here not so long ago. The hash is easy, the strained atmosphere more difficult to reproduce.

3) THE TOM AND DAISY SNACK

Nick Carraway the narrator glimpses Tom and Daisy in a rare intimate moment, trying to save their marriage—after perpetrating a hit-and-run road accident—sitting opposite each other at the kitchen table. Between them, a plate of cold fried chicken plus two bottles of ale. This is a special occasion, but not one that you would want to reproduce too accurately.

A Christmas Carol

THERE is no doubt that Dickens wrote with his stomach. When his characters have escaped from breakfast, they are preparing for another meal—and for Dickens it is often a celebration of some kind. In fact, he described the preparations for the Cratchit family's Christmas lunch in *A Christmas Carol* (1843) with so much loving enthusiasm that he has sometimes been credited with single-handedly inventing Christmas with this story alone. It is one of the best-loved stories in the English language, but it took him fewer than six weeks to write and nearly bankrupted him when he sued the publisher of a pirate edition. Even so, Christmas was never the same again after the tale of Ebenezer Scrooge, the four ghosts, and the dramatic moral transformation they caused.

YOU WILL NEED

- A GOOSE
- MASHED POTATOES AND APPLESAUCE
- GRAVY
- AN INFLAMMABLE PLUM PUDDING
- SOMEWHAT THREADBARE CLOTHES
- A HOT GIN-AND-LEMON MIXTURE ON THE STOVE
- A LITTLE BOY WITH A CRUTCH

COOKING THE GOOSE

The essence of Christmas in *A Christmas Carol* is the sense of occasion and the enthusiastic enjoyment of it. It may only be goose, potatoes, applesauce, and gravy, but this is not the time to invite comparisons—this is a literary feast, but it is also social comment. It is also absolutely impossible to follow the example of this lunch if you invite cynics to join you. In fact, even a small note of criticism will ruin it. Following the example of the Cratchits means swallowing every little bit of sentimentality—and ending the meal as you end the book, tearfully.

"There never was such a goose. Bob said he didn't believe there ever was such a goose cooked. Its tenderness and flavour, size and cheapness, were the themes of universal admiration. Eked out by apple-sauce and mashed potatoes, it was a sufficient dinner for the whole family."

~ CHRISTMAS CAROL ROLE-PLAY ~

The whole point about the Cratchits' Christmas is not that it is a sumptuous affair—it could hardly be that if you rely for your family income on an old miser like Scrooge—but that it was a great occasion nonetheless. It was much enjoyed, and everybody took part in its preparation, except possibly poor Tiny Tim. There are therefore three distinct stages to the Christmas Carol lunch and every one of them must be carried out for the experience to be truly authentic.

1) PREPARATION

The meal has to be prepared with great anticipation—mashing potatoes, sweetening the applesauce, straining the gravy—by all the guests. There are also some rather strange logistics that have to be undertaken for authenticity's sake. Like two of the Cratchit children, you will have to cram spoons into your mouths to stop yourselves from screaming for goose before it is your turn to be served. You will also have to dust the plates: in fact, dusty plates—dusty because they are rarely used—is a pre-requisite for this meal.

*"Two young Cratchits set chairs for everybody,
not forgetting themselves, and mounting guard upon their posts,
crammed spoons into their mouths, lest they should shriek
for goose before their turn came to be helped."*

2) EATING

There is really no possibility of any kind of critical note. This celebration lunch is the greatest one ever cooked with the greatest goose ever eaten. Only the hostess, the equivalent of Mrs. Cratchit at your meal, is allowed the slightest doubt—and only then about the quality of the flour for the plum pudding.

"A great deal of steam!
The pudding was out of the copper.
A smell like a washing-day!"

3) TOASTING

After the meal, there is still the hot gin and lemon simmering on the stove. The final stage of this lunch, therefore, not including clearing the table, involves gathering closely round the fire and toasting the health of everybody present and everybody not present.

"God bless us every one!' said Tiny Tim, the last of all."

A Piece of Pie

The sportswriter and war correspondent Damon Runyon used the title *Guys and Dolls* for his first collection of stories about life on Broadway, and when the musical version was made in 1955 with Marlon Brando and Frank Sinatra, they used the same title. But it was his third collection, *Take it Easy* (1938), that includes one of the most famous eating scenes in literature—the contest that takes place in the second-floor dining room of Mindy's on Broadway, to settle a wager about the eating capacity of the Boston eating champion Joel Duffle.

~ PIE LIKE A MANHOLE COVER ~

The theme of the story *A Piece of Pie* is that most of the characters have taken out substantial wagers on the competition, only to discover that their champion is not available. The contest is won by Broadway's champion Miss Violette Schlumberger—standing in for Nicely Nicely Johnson who is slimming down for his fiancée—but won by a simple trick. When she is seen whispering in panic to her coach on the arrival of the two-foot pumpkin pie, the Boston side demand to know what was said. On hearing that she wants a second pie before she even manages to start the first, the Boston side throws in the towel. In the event, coach and contestant run off with each other— but there is no need to carry the meal to quite these lengths.

YOU WILL NEED

- A STOPWATCH
- A CROWD OF BOOKMAKERS
- A RESTAURANT FILLED WITH KITCHEN STAFF
- TWO-FOOT PUMPKIN PIES
- EXTRA CHAIRS

THE RULES

Twelve courses of all-American food.

Each side to take it in turns to specify the dish and the quantity.

Each course divided neatly in half.

No more than two minutes' pause between mouthfuls.

Run-off using ham and eggs in the event of a tie.

~ A PIECE OF PIE ROLE-PLAY ~

Part of the charm of the meal in *A Piece of Pie* is the people taking part—the fifty or so roguish semi-gangsters and betting obsessives. Also of course the two competitors, Joel Duffle and Miss Schlumberger, who puts herself at an immediate disadvantage by forgetting about the contest and going ahead a little earlier with her regular meal of pigs' knuckles and sauerkraut. The menu is decided by the participants "of course," but if you are going to use Runyon as inspiration, you might as well follow the menu of the courses, each course divided into two.

COMPETITION MENU

1. *Two quarts of ripe olives, Twelve bunches of celery, and four pounds of shelled nuts*
2. *Twelve dozen cherrystone clams*
3. *Two gallons of Philadelphia pepper-pot soup*
4. *Two five-pound striped bass (not counting the heads and tails)*
5. *A twenty-two-pound roast turkey*
6. *Twelve pounds of mashed potato with brown gravy*
7. *Two dozen corn on the cobs*
8. *Two quarts of lima beans*

THE TRUTH ABOUT MINDY'S

Mindy's Bar, the scene of the eating competition and the haunt of Runyon's characters, was based on a real restaurant in New York city. Lindy's was opened in 1921 by the entrepreneur Leo Lindemann. Located on Broadway in the theater district, it quickly became famous for its sandwiches.

VALUABLE FOOD

What are we talking about here? One of the peculiarities of New York City slang in the 1920s and 1930s, the period that Runyon has immortalized, is the way that people used slang food terms when they really meant money. "Bringing home the bacon" meant—and still means—the wage packet, "dough" and "bread" both meant money. US dollar bills are green, which mean they also became known as "cabbage, "kale," and even "lettuce."

007 IN NEW YORK

If you are licensed to kill, is it really likely that you will spend a great deal of time eating, or that you have strong views about the best method of making scrambled eggs? Well, yes actually. James Bond goes so far as to describe himself in *Casino Royale* (1953) as "pernickety and old-maidish" in his obsession with proper cooking. He hates tea, which he believes caused the collapse of the British Empire, but his absolutely favorite meal is breakfast. Between them, Bond and his creator Ian Fleming seem also to have been responsible for the sudden popularity of the vodka martini in the 1960s, which Bond famously demands "shaken and not stirred."

~ THE PERFECT SCRAMBLED EGGS ~

In 1963, Fleming wrote a short story—the only short story he wrote about Bond—called *007 in New York*. It was published in the *New York Herald Tribune*, and its main purpose was to reassure Fleming's American readers that his hero was fond of New York, despite Fleming's article in the London *Times* which claimed that the city had lost its heart. This is the story where Bond sets down his opinions about his favorite dish, scrambled eggs. But he goes further: he provides the recipe. When anyone who is licensed to kill admits to a fondness for scrambled eggs, you feel a respect for their humanity and down-to-earth nature. Because the truth is that there is not a great deal of this in the Bond books.

YOU WILL NEED

- A TUXEDO
- A VODKA MARTINI
- SCRAMBLED EGG WITH HERBS
- LIGHT TOAST
- A CITY APARTMENT WITH A VIEW
- A SMALL REVOLVER THAT DOUBLES AS A RADIO TRANSMITTER
- YOUR LICENSE TO KILL

A GOOD READ DELICIOUS

CONVIVIAL (BUT KEEP YOUR EYES PEELED) TÊTE À TÊTE

Down and Out in Paris and London

George Orwell's real name was Eric Blair, and he effected a total career change at an early age by leaving the imperial police force in Burma to embrace socialism and writing. His first book, *Down and Out in Paris and London* (1933), opened up the seedy world of tramps and flop-houses, revealed from personal experience working in kitchens and sleeping rough in both cities. It was also this book that persuaded him to change his name, to make sure its revelations could not embarrass his parents living in a small respectable English town. From these small beginnings, Orwell was to become the influential author of *Animal Farm* and *1984* before dying at the age of just 47.

~ FAT, PINK FINGERS ~

So what is the special occasion? Well, perhaps not special, but certainly unusual. Throwing off your Etonian background in exchange for washing dishes in Paris or being shot at in Catalonia is not exactly run-of-the-mill stuff. For someone who deliberately puts himself whole-heartedly into the life of the underworld of tramps and grimy hostels, Orwell is amazingly fastidious. He describes some of the most disgusting scenes with loving horror, and for some reason it is the food that draws him every time. He reveals the same horror later, in search of the authentic working-class life in northern England, where there are the grubbiest corners of flop-houses and guesthouses to be dragged

YOU WILL NEED

- GRUBBY PLATES
- WAITERS WITH GREASY HAIR
- GREASY FINGERS
- GLASSES OF BLACK COFFEE WHICH NOBODY ACTUALLY DRINKS
- STEAK THAT HAS BEEN HANDLED BY THE CHEF
- A DIRTY BATHROOM

into the light. Orwell also enjoys a snobbish diatribe against the menu for tourists in Paris in the 1930s. This is not a culinary inspiration for the faint-hearted, but *de gustibus non est disputandum*—"there's no accounting for taste."

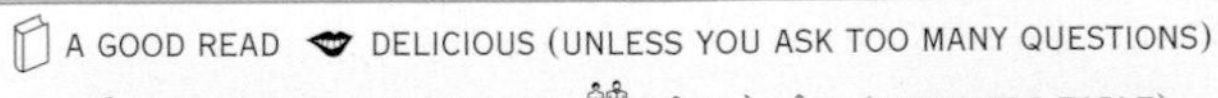

~ GEORGE ORWELL ROLE-PLAY ~

One of the more disturbing revelations in *Down and Out in Paris and London* is just how much the chefs in Paris restaurant kitchens in the 1930s manhandled the steaks, picking them up in their fingers and licking the gravy. Nor was it just the chefs: Orwell includes the waiters in his condemnation, whose personal hygiene is equally nonexistent. What is more, this is a symptom of culinary artistry, he says. The better paid the cooks, the more likely their customers have to eat what he calls "sweat and spittle" with their meal.

1) THE PARISIAN MEAL

Orwell paints a particularly unpleasant picture of one Parisian restaurant where he works in the kitchens among lettuce leaves, torn paper, and trampled food. He describes waiters with sweaty armpits mixing the salads and sticking their thumbs into the pots of cream. In the Hotel X, which he also describes, everything was sub-standard but expensive—the jam was cheap, the cream diluted, the tea and coffee horrible. But the guests were undiscerning.

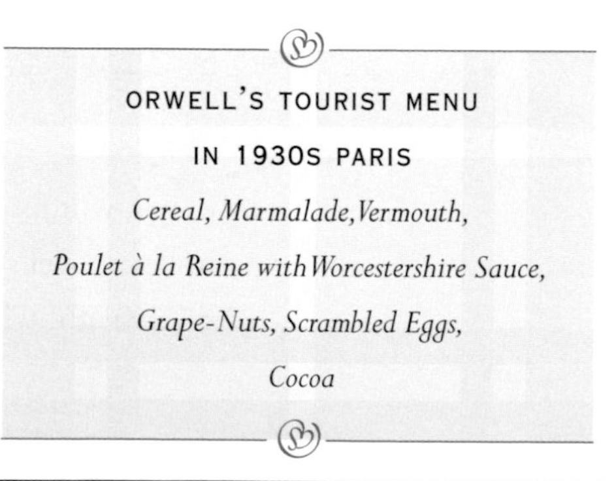

ORWELL'S TOURIST MENU

IN 1930S PARIS

Cereal, Marmalade, Vermouth,

Poulet à la Reine with Worcestershire Sauce,

Grape-Nuts, Scrambled Eggs,

Cocoa

2) THE WIGAN MEAL

Another meal best avoided is the one that Orwell receives at the hands of the Brookers, the couple he stays with in *The Road to Wigan Pier* (1936). Characteristics of the meal include: Bread and butter in slices, but always with a black thumbprint on each slice; tripe from behind Mrs Brooker's sofa; black beetles from where the tripe was kept.

3) THE ASPIDISTRA MEAL

Gordon Comstock, in *Keep the Aspidistra Flying* (1936), manages to eat rather better. Finding himself briefly with money in his pocket, he strolls into a pub and spends a total of 2 shillings and 11 pence (about 27 cents) on a meal of meat with two vegetables, plus a pint of pale ale, and twenty cigarettes. There is a certain nostalgic appeal to this.

4) THE PESSIMISTIC MEAL

Orwell's hero George Bowling in *Coming Up for Air* (1939) is characteristically pessimistic about the food he eats: a pint of beer and a pie that is colder than the beer, plus coffee and frankfurters, and the kind of tasteless stuff that comes out of cartons and tubes. Bowling's first taste of the frankfurter brings him to earth with a horrible bump. Not for the faint-hearted.

5) THE FUTURISTIC MEAL

If you are looking for the future of cuisine, you will have to hope it's not the one Orwell sketches in his futuristic novel *1984* (1949). Winston eats in the canteen at the Ministry of Truth, where only one beverage can take the taste away—Victory Gin. This oily drink tastes like nitric acid, but is the only beverage that is cheap and available.

THE CODE OF THE WOOSTERS

THE English writer P.G. Wodehouse began as a banker before turning his hand to comic writing of all kinds, even penning the lyrics to some of the songs in the musical *Showboat*. But despite writing almost 70 books in his long life, it is the characters of Jeeves and Wooster for which he is best known. What began as a series of short stories about an upper-class idiot and his brilliant butler grew into a whole series of novels written over a period of decades. In all these stories, Jeeves the butler is able to extricate Bertie Wooster and his friends from any number of embarrassing engagements and awkward situations. These are complicated by the interventions of his Aunt Dahlia, and her desperate attempts to keep the brilliant chef Anatole in her employ.

YOU WILL NEED

- A FRENCH CHEF
- AN ENORMOUS MENU IN FRENCH
- SILVER DISHES AND CANDELABRA
- CONSOMMÉ WITH APPLES OF LOVE
- AN IMMACULATELY GLACIAL BUTLER
- A SMALL PARTY OF CHINLESS WONDERS AROUND THE TABLE

THE PEERLESS ANATOLE

During *The Code of the Woosters* (1938), Bertie finds himself quite unfairly accused of stealing a small silver cow creamer, and it is only the thought of Anatole's cooking that makes the prospect of a spell in the slammer bearable. Before Jeeves works his magic and the threat is lifted, he sketches out the meal that Anatole will cook in his honor on his release, which he describes as a dinner "to live in legend and song." You will want to save this one for the most splendid occasion you can muster. Bertie Wooster regrets that he has only one stomach at his disposal, and although he sketches out his dream dinner, he does not actually have to go through with it: Jeeves is on hand to propose some simple blackmail to escape the clutches of the appalling and humorless accuser, Sir Watkin Bassett. One of the courses, the *Mignonette de Poulet Petit Duc*, was described by Bertie as "Le Bird of Some Kind avec Chipped Potatoes."

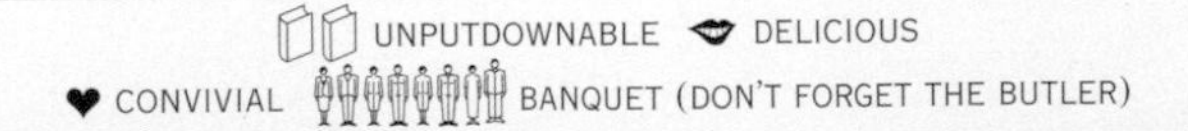

ANATOLE'S LEGENDARY DINNER

APPETIZERS

Caviar Frais

Cantaloupe

Consommé aux Pommes d'Amour

Sylphides à la Crème d'Ecrevisses

Nonats de la Méditerranée au Fenouil

Selle d'Agneau aux Laities à la Greque

MAIN COURSE

Mignonette de Poulet Petit Duc

Points d'Asperges à la Mistinguett

Suprême de Foie Gras au Champagne

Neige aux Perles des Alpes

Timbale de Ris de Veau Toulousaine

Salade d'Endive et de Céleri

DESSERT

Le Plum Pudding

L'Etoile au Berger

Benedictins Blancs

Bombe Nero

Friandises

Diablotins

Fruits

~ THE INIMITABLE JEEVES ~

The idea for Jeeves came to Wodehouse in 1919, wondering how he was going to get his characters—who were remarkably stupid—out of the terrible messes they tended to get into. His brainwave was that the butler would be a kind of super-hero. He named him after Percy Jeeves, an English cricketer. Jeeves appeared in print for the first time in 1923, and for more than half a century, Wodehouse continued with the stories—the last one appeared just before he died in 1974. Jeeves is always on hand to rescue Bertie with some subtle advice, like not to get married: "I would always hesitate to recommend as a life's companion a young lady with such a vivid shade of red hair," he says at one stage. Food is often uppermost in Bertie's mind, though Jeeves himself can rustle up an excellent omelet or, when appropriate, the most extraordinary concoction to deal with a hangover, the recipe for which is never revealed. If necessary, Bertie—and Wodehouse's other characters like Lord Emsworth and Uncle Fred—will also use food to help his friends: Bertie advises one of them that he should diet immediately to give the girl he loves the idea that he is pining away.

WODEHOUSE'S HAGGIS RECIPE

Wodehouse himself wrote famously about the Scottish recipe for haggis, implying that it was a method of lampooning your guests. It went like this: "The more intimate parts of a sheep" chopped up finely and blended with salt, pepper, nutmeg, onions, oatmeal, and beef suet. Resist the temptation to carry on adding things as a joke.

FURTHER READING

MEALS are a vital part of literature. They tell you about characters, atmosphere, and relationships. Events happen when people eat, and of course meals can be events in themselves. No wonder novelists, playwrights, and even poets find themselves writing endlessly about food. Not every culinary experience that plays a key role in literature has been included in this book, but perhaps it will encourage you to look a little more closely and smell the cooking when you are gorging yourself on the greatest writing in the world.

There is still a great deal to taste. There is Tom Bombadil's dreamlike entertaining of Frodo Baggins in J.R.R. Tolkien's *The Lord of the Rings* (1954–55). Or, more amusingly, Mrs. Gaskell's portrayal of eating peas with a fork in *Cranford* (1852). There are descriptions of eating as far back as Epicurus (301 BC), the Athenian philosopher who believed that pleasure is the only purpose of morality. Plato's *Symposium* (c. 380 BC) takes place at dinner. The list continues right up to the modern day, for instance *Primary Colors* (1996)—the novel by Joe Klein written under the pseudonym Anonymous—which provides a running commentary on the fast food diet of presidential candidates. There are also dramatic incursions into the politics of food by writers known primarily for something else, such as Leo Tolstoy's vitriolic vegetarianism, and Harriet Beecher Stowe—most famous for *Uncle Tom's Cabin* (1850)—complaining that commercial bread is "so light that [the loaves] seem to have neither weight nor substance, but with no more sweetness or taste than so much cotton wool."

Others use their views on food to beat those they dislike over the head—for example, Samuel Johnson complaining that the Scots eat the same food as their horses. Or to be especially cynical, Ambrose Bierce defining "good to eat" as meaning "wholesome to digest, as a worm to a toad, a toad to a snake, a snake to a pig, a pig to a man, and a man to a worm"—which neatly sums up the circular nature of biological life.

Further reading falls neatly into the category either of literary food or culinary history, depending on taste.

~ LITERATURE ~

Cooking by the Book edited by Mary Anne Schofield (Bowling Green University Press, 1988)

Food and Culture: A Reader edited by Carol Counihan and Penny van Esterik (Routledge, 1997)

Food for Thought edited by Joan and John Digby (William Morrow & Co., 1987)

The Oxford Companion to Food by Alan Davidson (Oxford University Press, 1999)

Word of Mouth: Food and Fiction After Freud by Susanne Skubal (Routledge, 2002)

~ HISTORY ~

The Cambridge World History of Food by Kenneth Kiple and Kriemheld Conee Ornelas (Cambridge University Press, 2000)

Cook's Books: An Affectionate Guide to the Literature of Food and Cooking by L. Patrick Coyle (Facts on File, 1985)

Dangerous Tastes: A History of Spice by Andrew Dalby (University of California Press, 2000)

A Food Chronology by James Trager (Owl Books, 1995)

Food in History by Reay Tannehill (Three Rivers Press, 1973)

History of Food by Maguelonne Toussaint-Samat (Basil Blackwell, 2001)

In the Devil's Garden: A Sinful History of Forbidden Food by Stewart Lee Allen (Ballantine Books, 2003)

Near a Thousand Tables: A History of Food by Felipe Fernandez-Arnesto (Free Press, 2002)

Tasting Food, Tasting Freedom: Excursions into Eating, Power, and the Past by Sidney Mintz (Beacon Press, 1996)

*"Miss Pole sighed over her
delicate young peas as she left them
on one side of her plate untested;
for they would drop between the prongs.
I looked at my host; the peas were going
wholesale into his capacious mouth,
shoveled up by his large rounded knife…"*

Mrs. Gaskell *Cranford* (1853)

INDEX